TEAM CREATOR

DON DURRETT

(Third Edition, August 2023)

Copyright © 2017 by Donald David Durrett
All rights reserved.

ISBN: 978-1-4276-5594-3

WWW.DONDURRETT.COM

Books by Don Durrett

A Stranger From the Past

Conversations With an Immortal

Finding Your Soul

Finding Your Soul Workbook

New Thinking for the New Age

Spirit Club

Last of the Gnostics

The Gathering

Ascension Training

The Way

The Path Forward

Get Healthy / Stay Healthy

America's Political Cold War

Post America: A New Constitution

The Demise of America

The Truth Shall Set You Free

(John 18:38)

Team Creator

Contents

Introduction v
Preface vii

Chapter One
   Gypsyland 01

Chapter Two
   Team Creator 17

Chapter Three
   Youth Movement 31

Chapter Four
   Party Time 55

Chapter Five
   On the Road 81

Chapter Six
   Harper 99

Chapter Seven
   Disclosure 109

Chapter Eight
   Free Tours 121

Chapter Nine
   Ted Talk 137

Introduction

I didn't want to write a book this year. I wrote *The Gathering* in 2014 and *Ascension Training* in 2015. I wanted some time off. However, when the universe or my higher self wants me to write a book, I don't really have a choice. They tell me over and over until I get the message. They are in my head, so they have ample opportunity to get my attention.

I don't believe that I write my books alone, so whoever is my ghostwriter for a particular book is probably the one giving me the most nudges. This book started growing in me a few months ago. First, the title came to me when I was updating the last chapter of *Ascension Training*. I got that "Oh no," feeling when it came to me. I thought that needs to be a book. I instantly said, "But I don't want to write a book." That was the beginning of the onslaught. Slowly, they began feeding me the plot.

I thought maybe I had an excuse not to write it. Surely, someone else had already written it? So, I went to Amazon.com and searched the book titles. No luck. Next, I Googled for a Team Creator website. I couldn't find a similarly-named website that was spiritually themed. "Ouch," I thought. Now, I don't have an excuse.

Someone needs to write this. I guess it has to be me. Being a member of Team Creator will change your beliefs and, thus, change your life. Moreover, it can help change the world for the better. It's an idea whose time has come.

One final comment, if you are new to newage/metaphysical ideas, read this as if it is fiction and don't take it too seriously. Your ego/beliefs are likely going to rebel against some of these ideas. If you rebel too much, you won't be able to get through it. And trust me, there is information in here that you want to know about.

Don Durrett 8/18/2023

Preface

It's 2027, and America has fallen on hard times, especially economically. Jobs are hard to find, and large cities have become violent, dangerous places. Many people have given up hope on America's resurgence. They have packed up their belongings and moved to makeshift small communities scattered throughout the land. It seemed like everyone was in survival mode, hunkering down to wait out this economic storm.

It wasn't dire. The Internet was still on, which allowed society to function somewhat effectively. You could still order from Amazon and get stuff delivered. Grocery stores, Costco, and The Home Depot were still open for business. The biggest change was that governments were broke, which curtailed consumer spending significantly. The unemployment rate was at least 25% for working-age adults in most cities, and not improving.

At least half of the colleges had closed, and perhaps a quarter of the primary schools. Many students were now home-schooled or used the Internet for online education. Roads were slowly degrading into disrepair. Hospitals were understaffed from a lack of funding. Most police forces only maintained a skeleton crew. To say that our quality of life had faltered was an understatement.

Team Creator

Chapter One

GYPSYLAND

Steve and Kate walked into their friend's house without knocking. They were expected. It was Saturday evening, and they had already made plans to visit. In fact, it was a usual event for them to visit Tony and Teri. They had been good friends for years.

As Steve walked into the house, he saw Sarah, Tony, and Teri's daughter, texting on her phone. She didn't look up. He waved at Teri and went into the kitchen to deliver some food that they had brought. As he opened the refrigerator door, he noticed Sarah's work. She had placed several signs on the door. The first one was a picture of the planet that said, "We love the planet." The next one said, "Spread the light," and another one said, "Join Team Creator." The last sign was something called the hand prayer that included several paragraphs in small type.

Steve went outside to the backyard, where he expected to find Tony.

Tony smiled when he saw Steve, "Hey, buddy. Glad you could make it."

"What else do I have to do?"

They both sat down and relaxed.

"Want a Kombucha?" Tony asked.

"Yeah, that would be great."

"I'll be right back. You like the green one, right?"

Steve nodded. "Yeah, if you have one."

Tony returned with two bottles of Kombucha and handed one with a green label to Steve.

"Thanks."

Steve looked at Tony but didn't say anything. He wanted to resume the talk they had last week and waited for Tony to figure it out.

"What?" Tony asked.

"I think it's time to go. Kate and I are ready."

"Cortez?"

"Yeah, California is done. It's not going to recover."

Tony looked at Steve and contemplated. This was a conversation they had been having all summer after Tony's daughter, Sarah, brought up the idea. She had become obsessed with a community called Team Creator in Cortez, Colorado. When she found out that her dad and Steve knew John Randall, one of the founders of Team Creator, she wouldn't stop talking about it.

Both families were what could be termed as newagers or lightworkers. They held metaphysical beliefs and didn't fit in with mainstream society. They only ate organic food and were either vegetarian or vegan, with an aversion to processed foods. Ecology and a love of nature were noticeable in the pictures on the walls of their homes. The reading material and books on their shelves were mostly metaphysical. An assemblage of crystals were littered throughout their homes, and the smell of incense was common.

"Are you sure Teri and Kate are ready to go?" Tony asked.

Steve nodded. "Yes, you're the only holdout. If we don't leave now, it's going to be cold soon. It's now, or we wait until spring, and I don't want to wait. Sarah said that we can join the new community that's being built next to Team Creator. Now's our chance."

Tony let out a long breath. "Okay, let's do it. I'll give my two weeks' notice on Monday. My sister can sell the house. When do you want to go?"

Steve practically jumped up out of his chair. "How about two weeks? Or do you need three?"

"Three," Tony replied. "Where are you going?"

Steve smiled. "To give everyone the news."

He hurried into the house to give everyone the good news. He was smiling. "Sarah! We're going. In three weeks, we will be living in Cortez!"

Sarah, who was sixteen years old, smiled brightly and gave Steve a hug. "Thanks, Uncle Steve." She knew that Steve had convinced Tony.

Teri and Kate both smiled, watching Sarah hug Steve. They knew how much this meant to her. She was a special child, who was gifted with amazing healing abilities. She wanted to go to Colorado and help heal people who came from all over the country. She had read about Team Creator's healing center and knew that it was her calling.

"What's that hand prayer on the refrigerator?" Steve asked Sarah.

"Oh, I got that off of Team Creator's website. It helps you to spread the light. You're supposed to do it every morning. You say it out loud, and it can include anything you want. Everyone can make up their own.

"The thumb represents who you serve, or who you work for. Where is your allegiance? The ego or your soul? The ego or humanity?

"The index finger represents when someone metaphorically points at you. What do they see? Someone who is selfish or selfless, an egotist or egoless, prideful or grateful?

"The middle finger represents giving the Creator the finger. Do you live the sin of pride as a hedonist, or do you live a life of purity and integrity?

"The ring finger represents unconditional love. Do you live from the heart? Are you kind, caring, considerate, and compassionate?

"The pinky represents a pinky swear to spread the light. This requires that we live God's virtues by remaining humble, grateful, trusting, faithful, selfless, and in service to humanity. We have to walk in the shoes of all the great avatars and saints. That's what is required to spread the light."

Sarah stopped and looked at Steve, waiting for him to reply.

"Do they expect everyone at Team Creator and Gypsyland to spread the light and live the life of a saint?"

"That's the ideal, but we know that men aren't as strong as women and probably can't do it." Sarah laughed.

Teri and Kate also laughed.

"What's so funny? I can spread the light." Steve said.

"Yeah, until some girl walks by without a bra, and there goes your plan," Kate said.

Everyone laughed.

"Hedonism may be wired into men, but it's also wired into women," Steve said.

"Perhaps, but not as strongly," Teri said. "All you need to make a man happy is sex, beer, and sports. Women are a bit more complex."

Steve laughed. "Okay, I'm going back outside. I can't win this argument."

* * * * *

"How much longer?" Sarah asked.

Tony was driving a Dodge Ram 2500 extended cab truck while towing a large travel trailer. Sitting next to Tony was Steve, with Sarah, Kate, and Teri in the backseat. They had stopped in Flagstaff, Arizona, the previous night; otherwise, it would have taken about 14 hours to drive from California. They had left Flagstaff at 8 a.m.

and had been on the road for about 4 hours and were getting close to Cortez.

"About an hour," Tony replied.

Sarah groaned. "This is taking forever." She, once again, looked down at her phone, while the adults enjoyed the scenic views of southwest Colorado. It was early October, and trees were changing colors. It was quite beautiful.

Tony and Steve had planned a long day. After they arrived and parked the trailer, they were going to drive to Durango and pick up another travel trailer that Steve and Kate had already purchased.

During the two-day drive, there wasn't a lot of talk, except for what they planned to do at their new home. Sarah was going to be a healer, so she didn't say much. Kate was an artist and hoped to work with some other creative people who made artistic products. She was hoping to make jewelry that could be sold on the Internet. Teri loved gardens and growing food and decided to do that.

Tony was good at fixing things and decided to volunteer as a handyman. Steve was good with computers, software, and programming. He would see if there was a need for that. He might even start a small company that made smartphone apps if he could find a few more programmers in the new community.

* * * * *

"The GPS says we are getting close," Steve said.

"Yeah, it's only about a mile away," Tony replied. "There should be a sign."

"I see it!" Sarah exclaimed as she pointed.

Off in the distance were two distinct groups of travel trailers. Tony slowed as he saw two signs that marked the entrance. One sign said Team Creator with an arrow pointing left. The other sign said Gypsyland with an arrow pointing right. He turned onto the dirt road and followed it. As he drove down the road, he could tell that this was the border of the two communities. When he got to the end of the road, he turned right into Gypsyland. There was an elaborate entrance gate, with a large Gypsyland sign above the entrance.

They could see about one hundred trailers and RVs, and a few buildings. They parked at what looked like the main building.

As they got out of the truck, someone came to greet them. He was a thin, white man about 30 years of age, with a long ponytail and a goatee.

"How was the trip? I've been waiting for you. Sarah texted me that you were due any minute now."

He held out his hand to Tony, "My name is Josh. I'm here to get you situated. I have two locations that you can choose from to hook up your trailer."

Tony, and then everyone else, even Sarah, shook his hand.

"Are you aware that we will have two trailers? Steve and I are going to Durango today to pick up his."

Josh nodded. "Yeah, I've been in contact with Sarah for about a month now. She has filled me in on everything."

"When is the orientation?" Sarah asked.

"We have one every day at 10 a.m. if someone signs up. I'll sign you up for tomorrow. It will be in that building, and it lasts about an hour." Josh pointed.

"Does anyone ever leave the orientation disgruntled?" Kate asked.

Josh laughed. "No. You will like living here. Nearly all of the rules are common sense ones that anyone would agree to uphold. Everyone wants to live in peace and harmony, but you can't do that with zero rules. Someone has to set the community standards. I think the model we have chosen works well. We're not as strict as our neighbor, Team Creator. They actually live by a written constitution."

"Yeah, I've read it," Sarah said. "It's not so bad. I could live there."

Tony laughed. "You're practically going to. You'll probably spend more time there than here."

"Why is that?" Josh asked.

"I have a job there to be a healer," Sarah beamed.

"Excellent," Josh said. "They have a very good healing center. We all use it. Both communities are very integrated. We do a lot of things together, especially business."

"Okay," Tony said. "Let's see those hookup spots."

"First," Josh said, "does anyone need to change their shoes? It's a bit of a walk. Also, I know you have been driving for a while. Why don't we make a quick trip inside, and you can get something to eat or drink. You can take it with you. I'll have a backpack for any trash."

"I need to change my shoes," Teri said. "I'll meet you inside." She started walking back to the trailer, where they had all of their luggage.

The rest of them went inside. There, they met several new friends and helped themselves to an assortment of drinks and snacks. All of it was free to those who lived in the community.

* * * * *

After about a five-minute walk down a dirt road that was lined with trailers, they came to the first location.

"This would be my choice," Josh said. "The views are excellent, and the sun will rise from that direction, giving you more direct sunlight. We can put solar panels on your roof, and it will be an ideal spot."

"Can we put both trailers here, side by side?" Tony asked.

Josh nodded, "Yep."

"I like it," Sarah said.

"What's our second choice?" Tony asked.

Josh took off his backpack and removed a document from within it. "Here is the community master plan. We always like to show newcomers the plan and give them the opportunity to select any spots that are available."

Josh laid down his backpack on the ground, and then placed the master plan on top of his backpack. Everyone gathered round. He pointed at the plan, "This is where we are now, and these are the spots that are available."

"It doesn't look like anyone lives over there," Kate said.

Josh looked at Kate. "There are a few trailers, but not many yet."

"Why would we want to live over there?" Steve asked.

"Only one reason. It will be quieter. The trailers are more spread out, but it's a longer walk to the main buildings and the gate."

"Why will it be quieter?" Kate asked.

Josh smiled. "This is Gypsyland. It can get noisy, especially at night when people like to talk or play music."

"I want to stay right here," Sarah said. "This is where everything is happening."

Everyone smiled at Sarah's assuredness and agreed with their silence.

"Okay," Josh said. "Let's get your trailer hooked up."

* * * * *

The next morning, they went to the orientation. It was held by two women, both of whom were in their mid-twenties. They stood in front of the room, while Tony, Steve, Teri, Kate, and Sarah sat in chairs that were lined up in rows, which seated about fifty people.

Gypsyland - Chapter One

"I'm Jane and this is Sue. We're going to tell you all about Gypsyland. First of all, welcome. We've lived here about a year, and it's really a fun place to live. Everyone becomes family very quickly as we get to know each other. Gypsyland is only on one hundred acres, so it's small. There are currently about two hundred people, and the plan is to limit the capacity to three hundred. Once we get to three hundred, we will let in a few more people, if they are family or close friends, but it won't be easy to get in, once we reach capacity.

"Until then, anyone is welcome, if they have a sponsor. If you are going to sponsor someone, we ask that you wait at least three months, so that you know exactly what you are recommending. Also, we ask that you only sponsor people that you know well, and who can give back to the community. This is not a retirement home. We prefer active people with some type of skill, and everyone is expected to be of service in one form or another.

"The main buildings are shared by everyone. They include the cafeteria, where you can get food twenty-four/seven. We have three cooks, but they set their own hours. If one of them is working, you can order off a daily menu. When they are gone, there are leftovers in the refrigerators. Everything is labeled, so it's easy to find what you want. The food here is good. You won't be hungry."

"Can we have food in our trailer?" Kate asked.

"Yes, of course," Sue said. "We have a small farm on about ten acres. The harvested food from the farm can be taken to your trailers. Also, we have storage bins of food in the cafeteria that you can take to your trailers. We usually always have some fruit in our trailer. I recommend that you only snack in your trailer and come to the cafeteria for larger meals."

"Can we order food from the outside? Like raw nuts?" Steve asked.

"If you have a credit card or Bitcoin," Sue said, "then you can order nearly anything online. It will be delivered to the building at the front gate."

"Next to the cafeteria," Sue continued, "is the laundry room. There are also showers and bathrooms in the laundry room. I don't think we've mentioned it yet, but everything is free in Gypsyland. Once you cross through the front gate, no money changes hands. There are no taxes and no fees. We make our money from donations from members, and the farm income. Once a week, we go to the farmers market in Durango and sell harvested food. Currently, we have about one million dollars in our bank accounts. Most of that came from donations."

"We plan to donate a large sum," said Tony. "As soon as my house sells, I will transfer the funds."

Sue smiled. "Thank you. That is very generous."

"There are a few items that are not free," Jane said. "If you want to own a cell phone or a personal computer, that is your expense. There is a nearby cell tower, and we get good access here. We have 5G Wi-Fi Internet, which is free. You can own your own vehicle, at your own expense. Lastly, any items that we do not have which you wish to purchase, come at your cost. If you need to borrow something, like a power tool or a sewing machine, you can do that through a request on our intranet website."

Jane looked at everyone to see if they had any questions, and then continued.

"Next to the laundry room is the entertainment room. It's actually four rooms. Three of them have large screen TVs, and the fourth has several cubicles with computers for Internet access. Each of the TV rooms seats about twenty people. They are popular at night. It's first-come-first-serve, and once a movie or show ends, the room votes on what to watch next. Democracy rules."

"If a TV or computer breaks," Sue said, "there is a problem box in each room with a pad and pen. Describe the problem on the pad and drop it into the box. You can also report problems at the front entrance if someone is working."

"We do not yet have an exercise or yoga room," Jane said. "However, you can use the one next door at Team Creator. We plan to build one in the future. We also do not have a healing building. You can use the one at Team Creator."

"That's where I'm working," Sarah said.

The two young women who gave the orientation smiled. "That's awesome. Hopefully, we can have our own healing center here one day, and you can work there."

"The last building is at the front entrance," Jane said. "It's used to welcome new people to the community, greet visitors, and take deliveries. If no one is there, we have a special texting doorbell. It will text people in about five trailers that are near the front entrance. Then someone will volunteer to help out whoever is waiting.

"We have two water wells, one that is used for the farm and one for the rest of us. We also have two large water tanks that are kept full. Nearly all of our electricity comes from solar and wind. We have backup batteries that can hold about one week's worth of our energy needs.

"The farm is our biggest function. If you find yourself without anything to do, there is usually something to do at the farm. We have several large greenhouses that operate year-round. We have a bit of a competition with Team Creator to see who can produce the best fruits and vegetables.

"On Saturday nights, a band at Team Creator plays music and has a dance. It's a big party every week and we are invited. You will also find people here that play music at night. It's a very festive community. We like to get out of our trailers and commune with our neighbors. Often, you will see groups of people hanging out together."

"Does everyone spread the light like they do at Team Creator?" Sarah asked.

Sue and Jane smiled. "Yes, it's why we are here. Gypsyland was created after Team Creator ran out of space. We were drawn here from what Team Creator started. They are spreading the light and so are we. The people here are all like-minded and live by God's virtues. We live in purity and innocence. We don't let the darkness into our community. We spread the light and hope that it spreads throughout humanity."

"Do you do the hand prayer?" Sarah asked.

"That is something that is recommended by Team Creator," Jane said. "Some people do the hand prayer, but not all. You will find that once you get into the habit of living God's virtues that it is not needed. Before I came here, I did it every day. On the outside world, the darkness is pervasive, and you have to work hard to keep out your personal demons. Here you will find that it is a much easier thing to do."

Sue smiled. "There is so much joy in this community that all you have to do when you wake up in the morning is acknowledge that you plan to spread the light. That's enough. You will feel the gratitude, and you will feel the love that pervades the community. You will find that the hand prayer is no longer needed."

"It's like doing your times tables after they have already been learned. It becomes meaningless," Jane added.

"Okay, one last thing," Sue said. "We have an intranet with a community website that is not open to the public, although it is shared between Team Creator and Gypsyland. We ask that everyone share their biography and post some pictures. And we ask that you read everyone's bio, to get to know them. Share as much information as possible. Include your birthday, so that people can check if they are compatible with you. We have a compatibility app on our website that you can use. The best way to find friends is to find people you are compatible with. Share your natal horoscope and other details like that. You might want to read a few bio's before you post your own, to get some ideas of what to post."

"I'm a five of clubs," Jane said. "I like to meet all of the other fives. I find that we all have something in common. Some of my best friends in both communities are fives."

"You make it sound like both communities are not just neighbors, but work closely with each other," Steve said. "Are there any rules that govern this integration?"

"Why didn't you just become part of Team Creator?" Tony added.

"Team Creator donated the land to Gypsyland," Jane began, "but they didn't want their community to grow any larger. They liked the harmony that existed and did not want to disrupt what they had created.

"So, we are welcome to come and go in their community, but we do not eat at their cafeteria or use their entertainment rooms. We do use their exercise and yoga rooms, along with their healing center. There is a degree of crossover, but we have remained distinct communities. We think it is the best arrangement, and it has been working out."

"You mentioned rules," Sue said. "Team Creator likes to write their rules down and use a governing committee. We are a bit more carefree here at Gypsyland. We do not write our rules down, but we do have a small leadership team. They pay the bills and make sure everything runs smoothly."

"What happens if someone has a complaint?" Tony asked.

"It would go to the leadership team," Sue said. "Luckily, we have not had to exile anyone, yet. We know, eventually, that will happen. They will be driven to Durango and told not to come back."

"Gypsyland is a bit more laid-back and easygoing than Team Creator," Jane said. "However, we are still strict in abiding by the philosophy that Team Creator originally created. We do not allow mind-altering drugs or alcohol, and we discourage any use of expletives. You will still find that there is a degree of laxity at Gypsyland that does not exist at the more pristine Team Creator."

"You could say that next door at Team Creator, they are all metaphorically wearing white," Sue added. "Whereas, here at Gypsyland, we tend to be a bit more colorful."

"So, basically what you are saying is that you could see or hear things at Gypsyland that you would not see at Team Creator?" Kate asked.

"Yeah," Jane replied. "The tone is a bit different."

"There is more reverence next door," Sue added.

"They are a bit more evolved, but we are catching up," Jane said.

"Does anyone have guns?" Steve asked, changing the subject.

"Yes, both communities have militias," Sue said. "We have to be prepared for some type of invasion from outside enemies. We can't be so naive as to believe we are living in a safe world. If you want to join the militia, it's on the website."

"That reminds me," Jane said. "The website has a lot of information about both communities. There is a blog, where various groups post. If you want to see if there are any job openings, that's where to go."

"We have our own mini-FaceBook, called MyCommunity," Jane said. "It was created by two teenage programmers at Team Creator. You will find that it is fun to use. Once you post your bio, you become part of MyCommunity. When the techs come by your trailer, they will show you how to log in to the Internet and intranet. They should be by sometime today. I already notified them that you have moved in."

"If I want to begin a small business, can I bring in another trailer to host it?" Steve asked.

"Sure, that's not a problem as long as the community benefits from some of the profits," Jane said. "We expect all money-making ventures to be shared by the community. You can determine how much you share. Some people give all of their earnings to the community, others much less. There is no minimum, but we suggest at least ten percent."

"Any more questions?" Sue asked.

Everyone was quiet.

"Okay, that's it," Jane said. "If you have any questions, you can find Sue and me on MyCommunity."

Chapter Two

TEAM CREATOR

The Team Creator community was located on 100 acres. It was outside of the city of Cortez, in a remote area that was accessed via a dirt road. Most of the 300 inhabitants lived in trailers, although there were 12 small houses that circled the main buildings. Inside these houses are where the original members of Team Creator lived.

One of these members was John Randall, whose idea of Team Creator was released to the world in 2017. The idea was simple to grasp for those in the new age community, although, perhaps, a bit esoteric for the average citizen. The idea was that the world was currently undergoing a spiritual transformation, and the Creator needed help with this endeavor. If you wanted to help in this undertaking, then you could join the team. To do this, you had to "spread the light," which was done by living God's virtues and being an example.

God's virtues were something that anyone could understand, but few could live. To be a team member was to live a life of being kind, compassionate, considerate, empathetic, loving, humble, grateful, trusting, serving, generous, patient, tolerant, non-judgmental, selfless, peaceful, joyful, and having unconditional love.

Those called to be team members were nearly all old souls. They knew what it meant to have deep self-respect for the soul and for the Creator. They knew that the most important thing was to act in love and integrity at all times, which was an act of selfless service to humanity. It was the opposite of living a life of pride and hedonism. Instead of living for oneself and one's pleasures, one lived for humanity and all of life.

A team member lived with an allegiance with the Creator because they recognized that they were one with the Creator, as was all life. They recognized that separation was an illusion and there was only one consciousness, which we all shared. It wasn't their job to spread this truth other than by being an example by spreading the light. It was their job to spread the light in such a consistent manner that it spread light to the world. This had the impact of steadily removing the darkness from the world. The team member's objective was to remove evil, violence, emotional pain, suffering, torment, trauma, and aggression, throughout the world simply by being.

Light and dark energies exist. They are not good or bad, but simply are energies. God does not judge, so there is no right or wrong. God doesn't judge, because God is all that is, and does not judge itself (for lack of a better word). God's core is love and perfection, which is also our core. It's who we are, and our true self. The planet had reached a point when it was time for the darkness to reduce in strength, and for the light to shine brighter. It was Team Creator's mission to help with this outcome, and spread the light.

In some respects, Team Creator's members were like devout Christians. However, a big difference was that members of Team Creator had no fear of God. They believed they were one with God, so the concept of fearing God made no sense to them. And because they believed everyone was one with God, the concept of judgment also made no sense. This allowed members of Team Creator to live any lifestyle they desired, as long as it was virtuous. Why virtuous? Because if God's core is love and God is perfection, then virtue and innocence are God's main traits.

From these beliefs, Team Creator lived in service to others, and not in service to one's self. However, that did not prevent them from enjoying the pleasures of life. While narcissism and hedonism were recognized as non-virtues, the pleasures of life were not abolished. In fact, enjoying life was, perhaps, one of their highest ideals. Everyone was expected to share their joy, and live life with gratitude and a smile. A love for oneself, God, and humanity was pervasive throughout the community.

It was recognized that on the higher spiritual dimensions, when we are not incarnate, we live with constant joy and bliss. That is our natural state. If God's core, and our core, is love, and we are perfect eternal beings, then joy and bliss would indeed be our natural state. For this reason, this is one of God's virtues. Thus, it is virtuous to be joyful and happy. It is what God expects from us. When we are not joyful and happy, we are not in an enlightened state.

Perhaps I should clarify the beliefs of the community. They believed in the concept of oneness, and that everyone was part of a singular consciousness. This all-encompassing consciousness was part of the Creator, and nothing existed outside of this consciousness. This made everyone not only connected to each other, but literally one with the Creator.

The concept of oneness was, by far, the most important belief held by the community. From this belief stemmed all other beliefs, such as reincarnation, and the belief that they were an eternal soul living in a human body. Each soul was on a long, long journey of evolvement. Everyone was on their own personal journey, and at a different level of spiritual awakening. For this reason, no two people held the same truths or needed the same lessons. Each person was unique, and each journey unique.

What created so much compassion and non-judgment in the community was the belief that all journeys led to the same outcome: enlightenment. Everyone was destined to become an ascended master, an avatar. Perhaps not in this lifetime, but at some point. The light in each of us would eventually come forth. Everyone was a piece of God that was evolving into something extraordinary, something beyond our comprehension.

Why the focus on virtue? Because to get close to our core, which is love, you must reside in truth and vibrate in truth. It must become your tone, your frequency. And the only truth is God's virtues. Peace is true. Love is true. Freedom is true. Gratitude is true. Compassion is true. These are the virtues that get you close to love and close to God.

The community did not have a church, or even a religion. Instead, spirituality was an individual experience. People did seek out spiritual guidance from the more evolved members, but it was highly encouraged that each member find their own truths and their own way. Accepting someone else's beliefs was not the path to enlightenment. Each soul had to find their own way, their own beliefs. This is what creates an evolved soul, a spiritually aware person. This is what makes a life worth living. Not to follow another, but to learn to follow one's soul, which ultimately leads to the answers we seek. You may not be searching for answers yet, but eventually, you will. And when you do, the answers can only be found within.

The community had its own constitution. It was based on a book titled *Post America: A New Constitution*. In the book, the author wrote a new constitution, in which all of the laws were created by volunteers. The volunteers were selected to serve for one-year terms by a committee. The potential volunteers were selected at random, just as we do for juries. Each year, the new government could keep the existing laws, overturn them, or create new laws. It was a self-correcting mechanism that prevented corruption and stagnation. It was literally a government by the people, for the people.

There was currently no taxation because the community had a large endowment, and people donated to the endowment. Many families had income from various professions and businesses, including artists, musicians, writers, furniture makers, and jewelry makers.

No money was exchanged inside the community. Everyone could eat for free at the community cafeteria. If someone needed something, such as cleaning supplies for their trailer or house, they could order it on the community website and have it delivered. The community also had several vehicles that could be used to make trips into town to purchase items, if one could not wait for a delivery.

A small farm, including several greenhouses, kept many members of the community busy year-round. The food grown on the farm was used in the cafeteria. They also had a juice bar, where one could get freshly juiced drinks. It was a very healthy community because of the focus on nutritious food.

The buildings in the center of the community consisted of a cafeteria, a healing center, a yoga/exercise center, showers, and an entertainment/Internet center. The healing center was large, with several rooms. Visitors from all over the country came to be healed, most of them for serious illnesses. They were treated using a large number of modalities, all of which could be considered holistic and esoteric. The most effective treatments were from different forms of energy healing. Many of the healers were young. In fact, age was not a factor in the selection of practicing healers.

* * * * *

John and Raymond, along with Raymond's son, Mike, hopped up into the commercial truck. It was a 16-foot truck with a tall, box-shaped enclosure in the back. They had purchased a used delivery truck and painted it green, since it was mostly used to take vegetables from the farm to the farmers market in Durango. They also used it for trips to Costco and The Home Depot to get supplies, which is what they were doing today.

They needed to pick up some lumber, to extend the size of the cafeteria building, along with a new freezer, two new refrigerators, and an assortment of smaller items. It was going to take some time to complete their errands, along with a stop for lunch. The drive to Durango was 50 miles and would take about an hour in each direction.

Raymond was driving, with Mike in the middle, and John riding shotgun.

As they drove down the dirt road to the main highway, Mike looked at John. "Mr. Randall, can I help build the new cafeteria?"

John smiled. "It's just an add-on, not a new cafeteria. Sure, you can help build it. You're sixteen now, right?"

Mike nodded. "Yeah."

"March fifteenth is your birthday, right?" John asked.

Mike nodded.

"You're an eight of diamonds. Did you know that?" John said.

"Yeah, sometimes we do compatibility readings at the youth movement trailer," Mike replied.

"I'm a five of diamonds and your dad is a six of diamonds. That's why we hang out together so much, because we are both diamonds. You're a diamond as well. So, the three of us are like peas in a pod. We are all compatible."

"What card is my mom?" Mike asked.

"Your mom is a three of hearts," John replied. "Most people who are hearts have a good heart and are very warm people. And because she is also a Libra, she is an especially warm person. I call Libras 'human lollipops,' because they are so lovable.

"So, while you love to hug your mom, you are actually closer to your dad, because you are both diamonds. Don't you find that you would rather talk to your dad, and that it's not always easy talking to your mom?"

Mike laughed. "You're right. I always talk to my dad."

"I think I have good news for you," John said.

"What?" Mike said, looking at John.

"I have a friend coming in from California. They are going to live next door in Gypsyland. They have a daughter named Sarah, who is sixteen. You're going to like her a lot. The good news is that she's also an eight of diamonds. I ran your compatibility last night on my *You and Me Compatibility* smartphone app. It was a five, which is a really good compatibility number."

"If she lives in Gypsyland, how am I going to see her?"

John smiled. "She is a healer, and a really good one. I've already told her that she can work at the healing center."

Raymond laughed. "Since when have you become a matchmaker?"

"This is the first time. Perhaps it will become a hobby of mine."

"Is she good-looking?" Mike asked in anticipation.

"I'll put it this way. You will have trouble talking to her the first time you meet her."

Raymond started laughing.

Mike looked at John. "Why is he laughing."

John smiled. "You'll find out."

* * * * *

The next day, Tony and Steve came to visit John at Team Creator. They walked into the entrance and were met by a security guard, who had never seen them before.

"Can I help you?" the guard asked.

"We live in Gypsyland. We're here to visit a friend," Tony said.

"Sure, no problem," the guard said. "I'm only here to help. Do you need directions?"

"He lives in house number four. It's supposed to be easy to find," Tony said.

"Yep, the houses are all easy to find. Straight ahead. Have a good day."

Tony and Steve continued walking down the dirt road toward the large main buildings. It was much more impressive than Gypsyland. Each trailer had been landscaped with plants and flowers. Many of them had fruit trees, and some had small lawns.

When they got to the main buildings, both Tony and Steve stared in awe. It was impressive. Completely made out of wood, each building was a piece of art. It was clear that the architect was also an artist. The window frames and door frames all were unique, with different carved designs. Also, on the outside walls were various engravings. It looked like the community had built the buildings together as an art project.

They thought about going inside some of the buildings, but decided to find John and let him give them a tour. They headed for one of the houses that surrounded the main buildings. There were flagstone walkways to each of the twelve houses, which were located about fifty yards from the main building in the center. It was obvious that the largest building in the center was the strategic point from which the houses were located.

As they walked along the embedded flagstones, they were impressed with the landscaping. It was a very beautiful place that showed a lot of work was being done to keep it well-kept. Plants, flowers, trees, and cut grass filled the central area between the main buildings and the surrounding houses.

On the first house they approached, they saw the number six painted on the front door. Tony pointed to the left, guessing that the houses were numbered in a clockwise manner. Sure enough, when they got to the next house, there was a five painted on the front door. A short walk later and they were knocking on door number four.

"Julie!" Tony exclaimed, seeing John's wife. She was in her mid-fifties, as were John, Tony, and Steve. Their wives, Kate and Teri, were still in their forties.

"Come in, you two," Julie said as she opened the door. "We've been expecting you."

They each hugged Julie as they entered.

"More like, you've been waiting for us," Steve said. "I think John always knew we would eventually end up here."

Julie smiled. "He's said that a few times." She paused. "But we're sure glad you finally made it."

"When John lived in California," Steve said, "he used to talk about building a community in Colorado. We didn't take him too seriously. Back then, the world was still a stable place."

"Yeah, he always said we would join him," Tony said. "I never thought it would happen."

"Where is he?" Steve asked.

"He's upstairs writing. He's working on a new book. I'll go get him."

Julie turned and headed up the stairs. "Find yourself a place to sit. I'll be right back."

The house was made out of wood and had a cabin feel to it. The floors, walls, and ceilings were wood. The furniture was very basic, nothing elaborate. It was not very big, although the main room was about twenty feet by twenty feet. It included the kitchen and main living area. There were two sofas and two large, comfortable chairs. There was plenty of room to host friends.

Tony and Steve found a place to sit, and waited.

John and Julie came down the stairs to meet them. Tony and Steve rose to their feet to greet John.

"John, it's been too long," Tony said.

"It's sure nice to see you guys," John said.

John hugged Tony and Steve separately.

"I like your place," Steve said.

"Have a seat, guys," John said. "Let's catch up."

All four of them found a place to sit.

"How's the book-selling business?" Tony asked.

"Not too bad," John replied. "I get some royalties, which I donate to Team Creator. The new age movement seems to be growing."

"Also, the Team Creator website and YouTube channel are bringing in a lot of business," Julie added. "After all, John is considered one of the founders of Team Creator. That publicity leads people to his books."

"Why do you think Team Creator is expanding so rapidly?" Steve asked.

"It's time," John replied. "It makes sense to people."

"Sarah, Kate, and Teri are members, but Tony and I haven't joined yet," Steve said. "How do we go about doing that?"

"It all starts with your beliefs," John said. "Do you believe that you are a soul, incarnated into a human body? In other words, do you believe that you are an eternal soul, having a temporary human experience?"

"Sure," Steve replied. "We both believe that."

Tony nodded.

"I thought so. I just wanted to make sure you understood that was the key. Once you recognize that your true self is an eternal soul, you are ready to spread the light. This is done by living God's virtues twenty-four/seven.

"You may ask, why would someone want to live such a virtuous lifestyle? There are two answers. First, we are living in a unique period of history when the planet is going through a spiritual transformation. This event requires volunteers to help with this process. We are those volunteers. Second, this lifestyle is actually the normal way of life for ascended masters. By following God's virtues, we are accelerating our spiritual evolvement. Thus, it is a good thing."

"Isn't the evolvement of the soul the meaning of life?" Tony asked.

John paused. "Well, I've read that the meaning of life is life. In other words, the perpetuation of life is the meaning of life. Consequently, our soul's evolvement does perpetuate life. So, the answer is yes, and making a conscious effort to evolve the soul is a good thing."

"I'm in," Tony said. "What do we do?"

"The best way to begin doing this is by saying the hand prayer twice a day. When you get up in the morning, and at night when you go to bed. The hand prayer will keep you aligned with your goal of spreading the light. Your hand prayer should evolve over time. I'll give you one that you can begin saying, and then you should modify it to meet your needs."

John got up and went to a desk that had drawers. He opened one of the drawers and removed a piece of paper. He came back and handed it to Steve.

"Here you go. Say this out loud," John said.

Steve looked down at the paper and started reading.

"Thumb: Who do you serve? Where is your allegiance? The ego, or the soul? Do you live by a deep self-respect for the soul and the Creator? What is your intent?

"Index: When people point at you, do they see a good example? Someone in service to humanity and surrendering to a higher power? A content, generous, humble, and grateful person?

"Middle: Do you give the Creator the finger? Are you prideful, living for yourself as a hedonist, narcissist? Or, do you live a life of simplicity, innocence, and virtue? Someone who is selfless, satisfied, and not attached to ego gratification?

"Ring: Do you live from your heart? Someone who is kind, caring, compassionate, with unconditional love. Are you sympathetic, empathetic, and not in your head, which is always ego-focused?

Stay in the heart and marginalize the ego. The heart is where you find your trust, faith, and guidance.

"Pinky: Do you live by the pinky swear to spread the light? Are you consistently spreading the light, increasing the brightness of your aura, while living in peace and joy? Living a life of equanimity at all times. Staying centered, balanced, and grateful."

"I think I understand," Tony said. "You don't want to chase after ego pleasure, because it is always temporary and never lasts. Pleasures often lead to addictions, which inevitably lead to heartache. True joy, like true love, can only last if you nurture it. How you nurture it is what gives you satisfaction."

Julie smiled. "Well said."

"What about your Saturday night parties? Aren't those hedonistic affairs? Is that still being virtuous?" Steve asked.

"It's a fine line," John replied. "I think God wants us to enjoy life, and that's why we have our Saturday night parties. However, the intent is key. Our intent is to share our joy with each other, and not live for ourselves."

Tony laughed. "You're right. It is a fine line. A good party is the epitome of a hedonistic good time."

"It doesn't have to be hedonistic," John replied. "All I do is listen to the music and talk to people. I go there to hang out. I can remain virtuous in that environment."

"I don't want to question what you are trying to accomplish with Team Creator," Tony said. "But it seems to me that you are sending mixed signals. The Team Creator concept is all about living a life of virtue and innocence. I don't see God as the big party type. That doesn't seem to fit in with God's virtues."

"Don't think I haven't thought of that," John said. "However, this is not a monastery. We are mostly newagers who like to enjoy life. The Saturday night parties seem to make sense. It's our way of bringing the community together to celebrate life. I don't think it is a big distraction from our mission of spreading the light."

"We don't think of it as a contradiction," Julie said, "although there are some people who will not come to the parties for that reason. But wait until you hear the beautiful music. Once you experience one of our Saturday nights, you will want to come back. They are wonderful, uplifting experiences. I feel more joy on those evenings than any other day of the week."

"It's a bit like the sixties, without any drugs," John said.

Julie nodded. "When you see those videos of California youth from the sixties, you get the feeling that everyone was having a good time, and love was flowing."

"Yeah, here it is more about being high on life," John said. "The love may flow a bit intensely on Saturday nights, but love flows most days around here. It's a joyful place to live. I wouldn't trade it for anything."

"Me neither," Julie said. "We have a community that is united in creating and maintaining harmony. The stress and competitiveness that we left behind are not missed. Yes, we have drama from time to time, but it is nothing like the anxiety that permeated our old way of life."

"It sounds like utopia," Tony said, with a bit of sarcasm.

"I wouldn't say that," John replied. "We live a simple lifestyle here, but you can find a high degree of happiness."

"That's true," Julie said, "although it's not for everyone. We demand that everyone live a life of virtue. We also demand that everyone contribute in some way. If you are a Christian or an atheist, then you might not like living here. But if you are a newager, who wants to add value to the community, then this might be your utopia."

"We don't ask a lot for what you get in return," John said. "We give you a community and a place to call home. For that, we ask that you contribute. How you contribute is your choice. As long as you are adding some value to the community, then no one will bother you. However, if someone simply eats our food and hangs out in their trailer, we can't accept that. That's not the community we want."

"What do you do, if someone won't give back?" Steve asked.

Julie smiled. "We show them the gate."

"They are exiled," John said. "Persona non grata."

"No bleeding Liberals here," Tony said. "Where is the compassion from the hand prayer I just read?"

"Everyone knows the cost of admission when they join, which is giving back to the community," Julie said. "If you want to be part of the community, then you have to join the community. You can be a hermit, but you have to come out once in a while and give back in some form. It doesn't have to be a lot, just something."

"What are some examples?" Steve asked.

Julie looked at Steve. "Working on the farm, working in the cafeteria, working on landscaping, working for yourself and donating part of the revenue to the community, working at the farmers market, working on cleanup crews. There are a lot of options."

"If you want to work once a week, that's enough," John said.

"What about retirees?" Tony asked.

"We try to discourage retirement, and keep people volunteering," Julie said. "The more active people are, the happier they tend to be. We only have one person over eighty at the moment, and she is still active. So, currently, we have no retirees."

Julie smiled. "I have no ambition to retire. I want to be active in the community until I die."

Chapter Three

YOUTH MOVEMENT

The next day, they began work on expanding the cafeteria's storage room. Four men and Mike began by laying a new foundation adjacent to the cafeteria building. They had an electric cement mixer, but they still had to make a lot of concrete by hand. It was hard work and would take them most of the day to lay the foundation.

Sarah walked by on her way to the healing center and noticed Mike. He stood out because he was much younger than the other men. She glanced at him, but he did not notice. When she arrived at the healing center, she was met by Michele, who was the leader of the center. She took Sarah around and introduced her to everyone who was working. Then they both talked for more than an hour about Sarah's experience with healing. After their long talk, Michele teamed her up with Alice, who used a similar Reiki energy healing modality.

Alice was also young, at twenty years of age. They both had success treating cancer and were of similar ages, so it seemed like a perfect match. Michele walked with Sarah to find Alice. They found her sitting at a table, reading her notes on a laptop.

"Alice, I would like you to work with Sarah. She has also had success treating cancer patients. You two should make a good team."

Alice smiled. "Sure, I'll take any help I can get."

"Okay, I'll leave you two to figure it out." Michele turned and walked away.

Sarah sat down. "What are you reading."

"I always take notes of my healing sessions. This is your first day, so I strongly urge you to do the same. Don't trust your memory.

Some of these cases can help you with healing others in the future. Plus, they can be used by other healers for their patients."

"What software do you use?" Sarah asked.

"We have a custom application called HC, which stands for healing center. It tracks all of our cases and provides us with patient histories."

"Very cool," Sarah said.

"Yeah, it's pretty nice."

"Do you have any patients today?" Sarah asked.

"I already worked on my two patients this morning. Toby is from Iowa, and Jonathan is from California. They've been here for a few weeks. I think I can send them home soon and work on them remotely. They both have cancer."

"Well, what are we going to do until tomorrow morning?"

Alice smiled. "We have a youth movement. Want to join?"

Sarah smiled. "Sure, what is it?"

"We answer questions online and post on the Team Creator website. We spread the word."

"Oh, I've used that before. I guess I'm already a member."

Alice shook her head. "No, we are the youth movement. We do it from here. There are about fifteen of us. I'm almost the oldest. Most are teenagers. Sometimes, we travel and give lectures. Sometimes, we create YouTube videos."

"Travel? Where do you go to?"

"Sedona, Denver, Colorado Springs. Mostly places nearby."

Sarah got excited. "I'd like that."

"You're in, girl."

They both laughed.

Alice closed the lid of her laptop. "Come on, let's go."

They left the healing center and started walking toward the youth movement's trailer. As they walked past the construction site where they were expanding the cafeteria, they saw Mike.

"That's Mike; he's part of the movement. Want to meet him?"

"He seems busy."

Alice laughed. "Not too busy to say hi."

"Mike," Alice yelled.

Mike stopped what he was doing and came to meet them.

"Hi, Alice, what's up?" He was dirty from working with the cement.

"This is Sarah. It's her first day. She's joining the youth movement."

Mike's throat tied in knots. He immediately thought of his dad and John laughing. Now he knew why. He almost laughed. His mind was thinking of a hundred things at once, but he couldn't talk. Finally, he blurted out, "Nice to meet you."

Sarah was the most attractive girl he had ever seen. He was instantly in love with her before she even had even said a word.

"After you get off, come and join us," Alice said.

"Sure, I'll see you then," Mike said, a bit more sure of himself.

"Nice to meet you," Sarah said with a smile.

They continued on their way, and Mike returned to the job.

"I think he likes you," Alice said.

"Why do you say that?"

Alice laughed. "I've never seen him that nervous before. He's too young for me. He's only sixteen, but he's perfect for you. Do you like guys?"

Sarah laughed. "It's my first day! And yes, I like guys. He's cute."

"I'll tell him you're nice."

Sarah laughed again. "Do you ever stop?"

Alice laughed. "Only when I'm working."

They both laughed. Sarah liked Alice, but Alice was more of a free spirit than she was. Sarah had a much more serious demeanor. They would make a good healing team.

They approached a large trailer.

"This is ours, the youth movement's. John Randall donated it to us. We have lots of laptops. This is where we will spend a lot of time hanging out."

Alice opened the door, and Sarah followed her inside. The trailer was custom-made, with more than a dozen small cubicles. These cubicles each had low walls, so the computer users could all see each other. There were several people inside, all of whom were under twenty. Alice waved to them as she entered.

"Hey, this is Sarah. She's going to join us."

Everyone nodded. Some of the kids had on headphones and didn't hear Alice. They took a glance at both of them and went back to what they were doing on the Internet.

"Come back here," Alice said to Sarah.

They went to the back, where there was an empty cubicle, and Alice sat down. Sarah sat next to her.

"Log in to the Team Creator website and go to the blog," Alice said. "Look for the youth movement thread. That's where we can help."

"How do we help?" Sarah asked.

"Read today's posts and see if anyone has a question. If they are online, you can send them a private message and ask if they want to chat. Many kids are interested in Team Creator, but they don't know what it's about."

"Let me watch you and get the hang of it," Sarah said.

"Sure. Bring your chair over."

Sarah moved her chair closer to Alice to watch her work.

"This one looks interesting," Alice said.

She opened a post on her laptop screen using her trackpad.

Sarah read the post. Someone was asking how to spread the light.

"They are online. I'm going to poke them and see if they want to chat," Alice said.

"What do you mean?" Alice asked.

"They will receive a private chat screen, asking if they want help with their question on Team Creator."

"Really?" Sarah said.

"Yeah, we can privately chat with anyone logged in to the blog."

"Their avatar is a butterfly, so it's probably a girl," Sarah said.

"That would be my guess, too," Alice said.

"She responded!" Sarah said.

Alice laughed. "Duh. They usually do. Wouldn't you want to chat with someone live at Team Creator?"

"What are you typing?" Sarah said.

"I'm asking her if she wants to use Skype video, or if text is good enough to answer her question."

"We can Skype?" Sarah said, surprised.

"You're slow, aren't you?" Alice said.

Sarah laughed.

"She wants to Skype," Alice said. "I typed in my Skype account. She will call us in a minute."

A few seconds later, they could hear the incoming Skype call. Alice answered and could see a young girl on the screen.

"Hi, I'm Alice at Team Creator. What can I do for you?"

"I want to join, but I'm only thirteen, and I'm not sure if I understand how to spread the light."

"Okay, well, I can help. Do you believe that you are a soul incarnated into a human body? A soul having a human experience?"

"Yeah."

"Cool, that's an important starting point. You can't spread the light if you don't know you have a soul to spread it with. Let me tell you a bit about the soul. If you could see it, there would be an assortment of colors. These colors are created from light. Thus, you are already holding light as colors. These colors represent the energy of your soul. Does this all make sense?"

"Oh, yeah. This makes perfect sense."

Alice grinned at Sarah, who was listening to her Skype call. "Excellent. Let me continue. The colors change, based on your beliefs and thoughts. You literally shine your light to the world, based on your beliefs and thoughts. John Randall, the founder of Team Creator, likes to say that our beliefs are our most precious asset.

"If you align your beliefs with God's virtues, then you can expand your light and share it with the world. This is what it means to spread the light. You are spreading the light at the highest idea of what you think God's virtues are."

"Oh! Oh, this is great," replied the girl. "If I do the hand prayer each morning and align with God's virtues, then I can spread the light all day long."

Alice smiled. "That's the idea. You will then be a member of Team Creator. Once there are enough of us, we will change the world."

"Thanks so much. I think you answered my question."

"If you have any more questions, just send me a private message."

"I will. Thanks again."

"Okay, bye." Alice clicked the disconnect button, and the Skype window closed.

"That was too cool," Sarah said.

"Do you think you can do it?"

"Oh, yeah. I was born to do this," Sarah replied.

They both laughed.

"Let's do another one," Sarah said.

"Sure. Do you want to watch?"

"Yeah, let me watch a few more before I jump in."

"No problem," Alice replied. She found another post with a question. "Here's a post from someone who is online. They don't have to be online, but I prefer to poke people with an instant message window, so that I can answer their questions directly, like we just did."

"Do you ever send private messages?"

"Yeah, if they aren't online. Otherwise, you can just poke them with an instant message window. One benefit of private messages is that they can be saved. In fact, they are saved by default. You have to manually delete them."

"And instant messages are not saved?" Sarah asked.

"Nope. Let me poke this one and see if we get a reply."

A few seconds later, someone responded.

"Two for two," Sarah said as the instant message box revealed an answer.

Alice started typing.

"Are you asking them if they want to Skype?"

Alice smiled. "You're catching on fast."

About a minute later, a teenage boy appeared on the Skype screen.

"Hi, Jason. I'm Alice. What can I do for you?"

"Are you at Team Creator in Colorado?"

"Yep."

"I want to come live there."

"Well, Jason, how old are you?"

"I'm seventeen."

"Do you have a driver's license?" Alice asked.

"Yeah."

"Okay, let me see it."

Jason left the screen and then came back and displayed it. Alice did the math to confirm when he would turn 18.

"Okay, you turn eighteen next summer. All you need is a sponsor and a trailer. You can probably buy a trailer for around fifteen thousand, used. Do you think you can save that much?"

"Yeah, I have a car. I can sell it."

Alice smiled. "Cool. Now you just need a sponsor. Team Creator is full, but Gypsyland, next door, still has openings, and probably won't be full by the time you turn eighteen. I have a friend at Gypsyland who could sponsor you. All you need to do is convince us that you are capable of being a member of Team Creator."

"What do you mean by us? Who do I have to convince?"

Alice laughed. "Good catch. You're pretty smart. My friend from Gypsyland is here right now."

Sarah moved closer to the camera so that Jason could see her. "Hi, Jason."

"So, just you two?"

"Yep. Convince us and you are in."

"Do I have to take a test or something?"

"This is the test," Alice said. "Or at least, part of it. We will have to talk to your parents and at least two of your friends. Is that possible?"

"Sure, but I don't have a dad. He left when I was seven."

"Sorry to hear that, but it's not a problem. We can talk to your mom. We just want to make sure that this is the right place for you."

"Okay, what do you want to know?" Jason asked.

"Tell me what you know about Team Creator," Alice said.

"It was created by John Randall a few years ago. The purpose is for members to spread the light so that the darkness on the planet can be removed. The more people who live with God's virtues, the faster the world transforms into a place of peace and love.

"Team members are lightworkers who spread light by their lifestyles, thoughts, and beliefs. These lightworkers work for the

Creator as a team that is committed to the outcome, which is world peace, accomplished through love and unity.

"Anyone can become a team member. The only requirement is that you live God's virtues. There are team members throughout the world, and it is expanding all the time. There is no such thing as a Team Creator organization, other than the example being set by John Randall and his community in Colorado. All team members are expected to be self-motivated and self-directed. We each work directly for the Creator, and that is our allegiance."

"Excellent! And how long have you been a member?" Alice asked.

"About two years now," Jason replied.

"Is this the first time you have asked to be a member?"

"Yes, I've considered asking before, but I didn't think I was old enough."

Alice laughed. "That's true. You have to be eighteen. Have you read any of John Randall's books?"

"Yes, let me grab some." Jason left the screen and then came back with a handful of books, which he showed Alice and Sarah.

"Okay, I see that you have read *Ascension Training*. What did you think of it?"

"I loved it. I've been doing the hand prayer since I finished it."

Alice smiled. "Good for you. Okay, you have passed the qualifications test. You are clearly an old soul. Young souls and mature souls have a hard time with that book. It exposes the ego in a way that is very discomforting."

Jason laughed. "That's for sure. Surrendering your ego identity to your soul identity does not feel natural. It feels like the death of the ego, which fights to remain alive."

Alice nodded. "Very good. John Randall calls it marginalizing the ego. It sounds like you have had success in this area."

"Yeah, I actually thought it was a coming-of-age test by God. If I wanted to know my true self, then I had to relinquish my ego. Once my ego was marginalized, all that would be left would be my soul."

"Did you find your soul?" Alice asked.

"Yes."

"Do you channel or communicate with your higher self?"

"Both. I think that's why I wanted to be a team member."

"Are you a medium?" Alice asked.

"Yes."

"Very cool," Alice replied. "Who do you channel?"

"Zander. He's Pleiadian. I only channel him once a week. He told me we should go slow with my studies. He's my teacher. I currently do not share his channels, but I probably will at some point."

"Does your mom know that you channel?"

"Yes."

"Good. How about your friends?"

"No, but they know I am into this new age stuff."

"One last question. Are you sure that your mom supports this idea of living at Team Creator?"

"Yes. She told me that once I turned eighteen, I could make my own decisions."

Alice nodded. "I think we are done here, unless Sarah has any questions."

"I look forward to meeting you next summer," Sarah said. "You can join the youth movement and help us spread information about Team Creator. I'm a lot like you, so I know how much you want to come and live here. Today is my first day."

Jason's mouth opened in surprise. "Your first day at Team Creator? That's amazing, and you're going to be my sponsor? There's got to be some kind of connection there."

"Probably," Sarah replied. "I have a feeling we are going to be good friends. Are you a healer, too?"

"Yeah, that's part of my training with Zander."

"Alice and I are both healers. We work at the healing center."

"No way! That's like a world-class healing center. You guys must be good."

Alice and Sarah both smiled.

"Train hard," Alice said. "Maybe you can work with us."

"I doubt it. We'll see," Jason replied.

Alice started typing. "That's my email address. Give it to your mom and two friends and have them each contact me. I'll set up interviews. We can use a phone or Skype, whatever they prefer."

"Will do," Jason replied.

"Any other questions?" Alice asked.

"Can we Skype again?" Jason asked. "I want to hear more about Team Creator and Gypsyland."

"Sure, if you see Sarah or me online, send us a private message to Skype."

"Great. I'll do it."

"Okay, bye," Alice said.

Once the Skype screen closed, Sarah looked at Alice nervously. "What if Gypsyland fills up by the time he gets here?"

"We can save him a spot," Alice said nonchalantly.

"How?"

"We are healers. We have influence around here. Do you know how much money people donate after we save their lives?"

Sarah shook her head no.

"Big bucks."

"Who do we ask?" Sarah said.

"I'll tell John about the call. He trusts me. If I say Jason needs a spot saved for him next summer, he's golden. He's in."

Sarah winced. "I watched *The Crown*. I no longer trust outcomes until they happen. Poor Princess Margaret. They broke her heart."

"Don't worry, Sarah. I'll take care of it. Besides, I doubt Gypsyland will fill up that quickly."

"I just don't want to break his heart. I know how much he wants to live here. Yesterday, I was in his shoes."

* * * * *

The next day Sarah ate breakfast and immediately made her way to the healing center. She was ready to begin working with Alice. After entering the front door and saying hello to Michele, who was seated at her desk, she started looking for Alice.

"Hi," Sarah said, after she found Alice in one of the healing rooms.

Alice smiled. "Good morning. Toby should be here soon."

"Do I need to get ready?" Sarah asked.

"Yeah, have a seat over there," Alice pointed to a desk across from her. "Log-in to HC and look up Toby's file. It's under his name, Toby Smith."

"Okay." Sarah did as she was told and began reading Alice's notes.

After a few minutes, she was done.

"I see he's making progress," Sarah said.

"Yeah, I think we can send him home next week."

"Maybe today," Sarah said.

"Why is that?"

"One of my guides said I can heal him."

"Who is that?" Alice asked, intrigued.

"Her name is Kiya. She works with me."

"Cool. I'll let you work on him, then."

A few minutes later, Toby arrived.

"Toby! Come on in and we can get started."

Toby closed the door and proceeded to take off his shoes.

"This is Sarah. She is going to work on you today."

Toby looked at Alice, surprised. "I thought you were going to continue working on me."

Alice smiled. "Don't you worry. If Sarah does not have more success than I usually do, then I will also work on you. Today, you will get a double treatment, if that's what is needed."

Toby relaxed. "Okay, that sounds good."

"Please lay down on the table, close your eyes, and relax," Alice said.

Sarah stood over Toby. She scanned his body with her higher consciousness, looking for signs of abnormalities. She knew where to expect them from Alice's notes, but wanted to make sure there were no others.

"Toby, I only see an issue with your thyroid. It's cancerous. I'm going to remove the cancer. You will feel the energy while it is being removed. It will tingle a little bit, and perhaps get warm."

Sarah held her hands close to Toby's neck. However, instead of removing the cancer, she replaced the deformed cells with healthy cells. It was more of a transformation than a removal. It only took about one minute because Alice had already restored most of the cells.

"Okay, I'm done. You can open your eyes."

"That's it?" Toby asked. "I'm cured?"

"I think so," Sarah said. "Let Alice check and see if it's gone."

Alice was stunned. She had been working on Toby for several weeks. She got up from her chair and stood over Toby. She used her hands to scan his body. When she got to his neck area, she scanned slowly over his thyroid. After about a minute, she stopped.

"Wow, I think you might be all better."

Toby smiled. "Cool."

"I want you to come back tomorrow, and we will check you out," Alice said.

"Okay, I'll come back at the same time."

Alice nodded.

Toby put on his shoes and made his way to the door. He turned to Sarah, "Thank you."

Sarah smiled. "You're welcome."

After he was gone, Alice looked at Sarah. "Is it always that easy for you?"

Sarah shook her head. "No, it depends on the patient and the illness. Toby not only believed that we could heal him, but he expected it. Plus, you had already removed most of the cancer."

"I still needed to do a lot more work," Alice said.

"Yes, but I have another level of consciousness that I can tap into. I could see a bit deeper into his soul's energy field."

"I was feeling puffy until just a few minutes ago," Alice said. "You totally popped my bubble."

They both laughed.

"Don't worry, we can work really good as a team. I can't heal everyone, and I can only work on so many people a day. The strength of my aura is weakened during healing sessions. What I did for Toby, I can only do a few times a day. Otherwise, I get really tired. Kiya told me that it is not healthy for me to get spiritually exhausted. I have to keep my energy level high so that I can help people."

"You mean that what you just did for Toby would not have worked if you had been spiritually exhausted?"

Sarah nodded. "Yep. It only works when my aura is strong."

"Okay, then," Alice said. "We will split up the workload to keep you energized. How many people can you work on a day?"

"It depends. For someone like Toby, I could probably do about five. But if it was Toby's first visit, then only about three."

"Got it. And if it was a really difficult case, maybe only two?"

Sarah nodded. "If I had to work on them for an hour, then maybe only one."

"How do you know when to stop?" Alice asked.

"Either I will recognize that I am getting tired, or else Kiya will tell me it's time to stop for the day.

Alice nodded.

Sarah smiled. "When is your second patient due?

"So, that's how it is?" Alice said sardonically. "You're going to steal all of my patients."

Sarah laughed. "No, I'm the new girl. I just do what I'm told."

"Well, I'm not going to stop you from healing people. I saw what you just did."

"I have an idea," Sarah said. "After I read your notes about Toby, my higher consciousness knew what to look for and what to expect. It gave me confidence when I confirmed your diagnosis. Why don't you do the first healing session, or first few sessions, and get the diagnosis and initial treatments done. Then I'll do a session and see if I can do the cure."

Alice smiled. "That sounds good. Why don't you read my notes on Jonathan, and you can work on him today. I think his diagnosis is solid."

Sarah sat down at her desk and started reading about Jonathan. After she finished, she turned to Alice. "I think I can help him."

"Excellent, we're going to be out of here early today."

"The youth movement trailer?" Sarah asked.

"Yeah, but first, we're going to visit Maddie. She's my best friend. You should meet her. She is nineteen, and also a member of the youth movement."

"Okay, that will be fun."

"She grows food in the greenhouses. She has a green thumb."

Sarah started typing on her laptop keyboard.

"What are you typing?" Alice asked.

"Entering my notes for Toby's visit."

Alice smiled. "Excellent. It's important to document each healing session into the HC database."

"When do you think Jonathan will arrive?" Sarah asked.

"In about thirty minutes. He's due at ten."

After Jonathan arrived, Sarah re-balanced his energy field, which effectively healed him. She entered her notes into the database, and then they were ready to leave.

* * * * *

They walked to the farm and the greenhouses, which were located at one end of Team Creator's land. Its location was away from the trailers and the houses because they used fertilizer and some natural pesticides to prevent infestations. They also had a tractor that was noisy.

They entered one of the large greenhouses, looking for Maddie. It was bright inside from the numerous lights on the ceiling. There were plants and fruit trees everywhere Sarah looked. She was stunned at the abundance of food. She wanted to get a bag and begin picking fruit, but knew that wasn't likely permitted. Harvesting was likely done on a scheduled basis and not randomly. Everything was too organized at Team Creator to allow for randomness.

There were two aisles, with numerous plants growing on each side of the aisles. There were also plants growing up the walls to the fifteen-foot-high ceilings. Dozens of fruit trees grew between the aisles in large planters. It appeared that each tree easily could be transplanted if that was desired. However, most of these trees would likely die outside in the harsh Colorado winters.

They walked up one of the aisles, looking for Maddie. They could not see the end because of the vegetation. Once they walked partially down the aisle, they saw a few people toward the end of the greenhouse.

Alice did not see Maddie. "Do you know where Maddie is?" she asked the people working at the end.

"She is next door in greenhouse number two," someone replied. "This greenhouse is number one. They are marked right above the door."

"Okay, thanks," Alice said.

They turned around and walked out. Sarah could not believe how tomatoes, green beans, and broccoli could grow without soil. But there they were, growing in the air, as if suspended from the ground.

"How much trouble will we get in if we pick something?" Sarah asked.

"Don't even think about it, girl," Alice said. "It's not ours until it is picked."

"That's what I thought," Sarah said.

They walked to the next greenhouse. It was just as huge as the first one, with solar panels covering the roof. Once they approached the entrance, they could see the number two above the doors. This time when they entered, they saw fruit being grown in individual buckets, which were stacked in layers. There were hundreds of cantaloupes, watermelons, and honeydew being grown. They also had racks of strawberries growing to the ceiling. There was no soil. It was almost as if they prohibited soil or did not require it.

Maddie saw them enter and came to join them.

"Hi, Alice, what's up?"

"This is Sarah. I wanted you to meet her. She is working with me at the healing center."

Maddie took off her gloves and extended a hand to Sarah. "I would hug you, but I'm a bit dirty."

Sarah smiled and shook her hand. "Nice to meet you."

"She lives next door at Gypsyland," Alice said. "Her family just arrived."

"Can my mom work with you?" Sarah asked. "I know that Gypsyland has a farm too, but she would really dig these greenhouses. Her name is Teri. You'll like her."

Maddie started to say something, but Alice interrupted her. "Let me talk to John," Alice said, looking at Maddie. "I think I can make it happen."

Maddie looked surprised.

"I know that it is not normal protocol to allow Gypsyland residents to work in the greenhouses," Alice said. "But Sarah isn't normal."

Maddie continued to look surprised. "What do you mean?"

"She's a very special healer. She cured two people of cancer today. We have amazing healers at Team Creator, but she is the best that I have seen."

Maddie smiled. "Talk to John. He might say yes."

Alice turned to Sarah. "I'll get your mom in."

"She might not even want it. Let me ask her first."

"Sure, let me know," Alice said.

"Where's the soil?" Sarah asked Maddie.

Maddie laughed. "We don't need it. It's called hydroponics. We add the minerals necessary for growing into the water."

"Very cool," Sarah said.

"We're heading over to the youth movement trailer," Alice said. "I got Sarah to join yesterday. So, you might see her there."

"I look forward to it," Maddie said. "I'll see you at the Saturday night parties, too. You can't skip those. The music is too good."

"She wants to dance with Mike, anyway," Alice said mischievously.

Maddie smiled. "You just got here, and you already have a boyfriend?"

48

Sarah pointed at Alice. "One of these days...."

They all laughed. The three new friends had just bonded for life.

Sarah and Alice turned to go.

"Tell your mom that I would love to work with her, if John says it's okay," Maddie said.

Sarah looked back with a smile. "I'll tell her."

* * * * *

Sarah and Alice spent the rest of the day hanging out at the youth movement trailer, talking and answering blog post questions. In the afternoon, Mike came in after he had cleaned up from work. He came to the back of the trailer, where they were, and found a place to sit.

"What's up?" Mike said.

"You're up," Alice said.

"What does that mean?" Mike asked.

"Well, we were bored, and now you're here," Alice said.

"I'm supposed to entertain you?" Mike queried.

"Yeah, why not?"

"What did you have in mind?"

"Let's do compatibility testing," Alice said.

Sarah laughed. "She never stops, does she?"

Mike laughed. "That's why we love her."

"What kind of compatibility testing?" Sarah asked.

"I know exactly what she is going to do. We've done this before," Mike said.

"Okay, who do we do first?" Alice asked.

"You two," Mike said.

"That would be boring," Alice said. "Why not you two?"

"Fine," Mike said. "You probably planned this last night."

"She probably planned this when we met," Sarah said.

Mike laughed. "I see you have her figured out, too."

"Okay, turn on the screen," Alice said, ignoring their comments.

Mike got up and turned on the big screen on the wall. Immediately, Alice's laptop screen displayed on the wall screen.

"Which one should we do first?" Alice asked.

"*You and Me Compatibility*," Mike said. "We can use that to do everything else, and it's a good starting point."

Alice opened the program. She typed in Mike's name and date of birth, and then Sarah's.

"Is that correct? I got it off the website," Alice said.

Sarah and Mike nodded.

Alice clicked a button and results came up.

"Wow, you guys are a good match," Alice said. "A five compatibility. That's amazing. Your lifepaths are a natural match. Your cards are a match, and your sun signs are a match. All of your numbers are matching or neutral. It's very rare to see a five compatibility. I've never had one with anybody. I think I had a four once. It's usually ones or twos. I consider a two a good match."

"What am I reading?" Sarah asked.

"This app is on our website," Alice said. "It was created by John Randall. You will have to do some studying to read it effectively. It uses numerology, astrology, and the science of the cards."

"I only know a little bit of astrology," Sarah said.

"Don't worry, I'll teach you," Alice said.

"Mike, I'll give you the honors. Please read it for Sarah."

"You have a nine lifepath. That's pretty powerful. Nines are usually leaders of some type. They also tend to be mature and strong. They're not the type of people you can push around. I have a three lifepath. As Alice said, our lifepaths are a natural match. Nine's and three's tend to get along. I respect your strength, and you respect my creativity, which is the common trait for three's.

"Our cards are the same. We are both eight of diamonds. This makes us very similar people. It's like seeing a twin of yourself. Sometimes, people who are married with the same card are reincarnated soul mates.

"Having a nine lifepath in tandem with an eight card is very powerful. When you combine that with your sun sign of Scorpio, you have a very powerful combination. I consider Scorpio to be one of the most powerful signs."

"Now we know how she cured two people with cancer today," Alice said.

Mike looked at Sarah and then at Alice for confirmation. "Really?"

Alice nodded.

Mike whistled. "Wow. That's amazing."

"Tell her the good part!" Alice said, not being able to contain herself.

"I know what she wants me to say, but let's not get ahead of ourselves," Mike said with a calm demeanor.

"Our card is a diamond," Mike continued. "From a compatible standpoint, people with the same card type tend to get along. Diamonds tend to be people of depth and a bit complex. They are also creative, independent, and philosophical.

"Alice, on the other hand, is a spade. People who are spades tend to be the most mature, and often the smartest, but not always the warmest. She is a Gemini, so her brain goes one hundred miles an hour, and she was born June first, which is a three of spades."

"I also have a three lifepath, making me compatible with both of you. But enough about me, would you please get to the good stuff?"

"Okay, now for the good stuff. I'm a Pisces and you are a Scorpio. We are both water signs. When you combine the fact that we have the same card, and a natural match lifepath, our compatibility is off the charts."

"I don't get it. Why are you both so excited?" Sarah said.

Mike looked at Alice. "She doesn't know."

Alice looked at Sarah. "Your compatibility implies that you are soul mates. That's why we are excited."

"How can you know?" Sarah said skeptically.

Alice burst out laughing. "You can heal cancer, but you are clueless when it comes to compatibility?"

"I'm only sixteen. I'm supposed to know everything?"

"You will. We're going to teach you," Alice said.

"Can I have the crash course, so I can understand why you think we are so compatible?"

"We don't think you are," Alice said seriously. "We know it. This is an amazing reading. You have the same card, a natural match lifepath, and your sun signs match. Plus, none of your numbers are incompatible. Considering your age and the fact that God brought you two together, if you're not soul mates, then God has a strange sense of humor."

"Is this rare?" Sarah asked.

"I've run at least one hundred compatibility tests," Alice said. "I've never seen a better match. John and Julie Randall are pretty good, but not this good."

"Me, neither," Mike said. "Now I know why Mr. Randall told me that I should meet you. He said that he had run our compatibility."

"What!" Alice exclaimed. "Why would he do that?"

Everyone was quiet, in contemplation.

"We'll have to ask him," Sarah finally said.

Alice nodded. "Okay. I want to be there for that answer. Let's do it together at the party Saturday night."

Sarah and Mike nodded.

"In the meantime, you have some reading to do," Alice said to Sarah. "We need to rectify your educational limitations."

Alice stood up. "Come with me. We're going to the library."

They started walking out of the trailer.

"Are you coming, Mike?" Alice said.

"Sure, wait up."

Once they got to the Team Creator library, Alice grabbed several books on astrology, numerology, and the science of the cards. She signed for each of them since Sarah was from Gypsyland. The library was not shared between the two groups.

Once they left the building with the library, Alice handed Sarah the books.

"Cover to cover, girl," Alice said.

"That's not fair," Mike said. "You can skip around. These books are too dense to read cover to cover."

"Okay, I suppose he is right," Alice said. "You can skip around, but make sure to read the sun sign and lifepath descriptions several times. And I plan to quiz you."

Sarah and Mike laughed.

"When are the books due?" Sarah asked.

"One month, and then they will come looking for me."

"Can't I download digital versions?" Sarah asked.

"You can try to find free versions, but the science of the cards isn't free."

"Okay, I'll read that one first. I think I can find digital versions for astrology."

"Good, I'm glad you're motivated," Alice said.

"She's an eight of diamonds with a nine lifepath. Unstoppable," Mike said.

They all laughed.

Chapter Four

Party Time

On Saturday, at Team Creator, they started setting up the tables for the buffet around three p.m. If there was a chance of rain or snow, then they would put up a large tent that was open on the sides. The tent was basically a large roof that kept out the rain or snow. They never skipped the Saturday night buffet, which was always followed by music and a party atmosphere.

Ever since Gypsyland had come into existence, they were welcome to join the Team Creator buffet and party, and most of them did. The main reason they came was for the food. While the majority of people were vegetarians or vegans, the buffet included barbecued chicken. There was a wide variety of food, and all were delicious. You could get Indian, Mexican, Italian, plus several others. The buffet was the food treat of the week.

The tables were set up in parallel lines next to the cafeteria. Each table could seat about eight people. They would line up four tables in a row, creating a section to seat 32 people. There were 20 sections, with two sections paired together to create an extended row. This created ten extended rows and made it easy to walk among the sections. They always set it up the same way, so everyone knew how to get around.

There was just enough room to set up the tables between the surrounding houses and main buildings. The paired sections were separated by a walkway to one of the houses. This had the effect of using the walkway to find a place to sit down. At night, the walkway had lights that lit up the area. The visitors who were there for healing always found it intriguing how everything fit just right. It was evident that someone had planned it in advance.

It was a bit of work to carry all of the tables and chairs from storage. Each week, people volunteered to show up at three p.m. and help. First, they set up the tables, and then the chairs. The removal took place the following morning. They found that it was better to do the removal in the morning because people had more energy. Also, there was less of a chance for a possible injury doing it during daylight.

Another group of volunteers set up the band stage and dance floor. This actually took longer to do than setting up the table and chairs. The dance floor was large and had to be put together like a puzzle. The band stage was raised and required that a metal floor be assembled. It required some tools and did not snap together easily. The stage required a degree of sturdiness and stability that could handle band equipment and several people jumping up and down. Plus, they had to set up the loudspeakers and wire the stage for the electric instruments. It was actually a fairly elaborate process. The volunteers who did this called themselves the roadies, even though they never took this stage on the road.

They started the barbecue at four p.m. The buffet line opened at five p.m. and remained open until seven p.m. At eight p.m., the music and dancing started and lasted until ten. Sometimes, the Team Creator band played the entire time, and sometimes, a deejay played recorded music.

The Team Creator band was constantly growing in size because of new people arriving. While not all of the Team Creator band was on stage at the same time, they would trade off playing songs. Also, the songs determined how many members were on stage at a time. Sometimes, there were four, and sometimes as many as ten.

Being in the band was considered a profession, and for many of the band members, that is all they did. They were skilled professionals and recorded some of their songs. They sold their music on the Internet. This was not a garage band. They were very

Party Time - Chapter Four

good. Having an audience to play for once a week kept them sharp and constantly looking for new material.

* * * * *

At five p.m., people started arriving. Tony, Steve, Kate, Teri, and Sarah all walked over together from Gypsyland. After they went through the buffet line and found a place to sit, Sarah waved goodbye.

"Bye, I'm sitting with my friends," Sarah smiled as she walked away.

Alice had told her that the youth movement all sat together in two reserved sections. They had placed youth movement signs on two of the paired tables in the back. These were located the furthest away from the cafeteria and barbecue. They liked sitting in the back as the rebellious group. Usually, the band would sit in the section next to them and join the rebels, away from the adults.

Sarah found Alice and Maddie and sat down with them.

"Woo-woo, it's Saturday night," Maddie said.

"Dancing time!" Alice said.

"I don't know if I want to dance," Sarah said seriously.

"Why not," Alice said.

"I'm not in the mood."

"It's not for two more hours. You might change your mind," Alice said.

"It doesn't feel right," Sarah said.

"What do you mean?" Maddie asked.

"I've been doing the hand prayer and consciously marginalizing my ego. I've been trying to get really close to my soul this week. I don't want Sarah, my ego personality, to seek out ego gratification. I came here to be a lightworker, and not to have fun."

Alice let out a long sigh. "I'll go get John. We could try to explain, but I think you need to hear it from him."

Alice got up and went to find John. They both returned a few minutes later and sat down next to Maddie and Sarah.

"Hi Maddie, Sarah. May I be of assistance?" John looked at Maddie and then Sarah.

"Sarah thinks that dancing is too hedonistic," Maddie said. "She doesn't want her ego to get in control and block her intent of being a lightworker."

"Yes, that is what Alice told me," John replied.

Sarah looked at John. "Satisfying my ego doesn't seem to be in alignment with my objective of marginalizing the ego."

John nodded. "I see your dilemma. Marginalizing the ego and living God's virtues is a laudable path, and one worth pursuing. You think that dancing is contradictory to these objectives. However, the ultimate goal of life is to evolve the soul. This is accomplished by living a life of deep respect and a life of love, for both yourself and others, as well as the Creator, the universe, and humanity.

"Dancing and enjoying life are not in contradiction to this ultimate goal. In fact, going counter to enjoying life is, perhaps, going counter to the ultimate goal. God wants us to love each other and share our joy with each other. Sitting and watching others dance, or staying home and not joining in the community celebration is, perhaps, counter to this goal."

Sarah listened intently, but did not reply, waiting for John to continue.

"We should use all opportunities to share our love with each other. The world is currently coming together into a form of unity consciousness, where there is cooperation and compassion. We are trying to come together and remove the separation that breaks us apart. Dancing heals us and brings us together. It is an act of love, and an act of joy.

"The action of non-judgment is an act of love. The action of respect for others is an act of love. The action of being gentle to others is an act of love. The act of sharing with others is an act of love. The act of joy is an act of love. The act of peace is an act of love. These are all God's virtues made manifest, and they can all occur when dancing. A simple smile while dancing is an act of love.

"We are here at Team Creator to share our love and to respect others, but also to respect the Creator and our soul. If we thought that dancing was counter to this objective, it would not be a significant event that we do every week. Self-love, self-joy are not counter to our objective. Just remember that this self-love is of the soul and not of the ego. We are letting the spark of God come out when we share our joy.

"We have a saying here that if you can't love yourself, then you can't love others. Self-love is required before you can love another. And what better way to show that you love yourself than to dance!

"We need to become aware of our true self and honor it. Our self-love is our love for our eternal self. This self-love then allows us to love others. We can then sense the amazing soul that exists inside of someone. We can relish in that understanding and celebrate that understanding through dance. It is a celebration of life."

Sarah smiled. "I think I understand."

Alice looked at Sarah. "Good. Do you get that dancing is spiritually healthy?"

Sarah smiled. "I do."

Maddie let out a sigh, "Thank God."

John smiled. "So, we're all good?"

They all nodded.

"Great," John replied, "but don't ask me to dance. I'm over fifty, and I only dance on my birthday and anniversary because my wife makes me. I loved to dance when I was younger, but I have lost my rhythm. Now I just watch."

They all laughed, and John got up to leave.

"Wait," Maddie said, "we have a couple of other questions."

John sat back down.

"Can Sarah's mom work in Team Creator's greenhouses?" Alice asked.

John thought for a moment. "Yes, but on two conditions. First, she needs to work in Gypsyland's greenhouses for a month before coming over, so that she will understand the differences between us. Second, she can only work for one year as an apprentice under Maddie. Then she has to go back to Gypsyland and teach them what she learned."

Maddie nodded. "Sounds good. That way they can catch up with us."

"Anything else?" John asked.

"Yeah, Sarah and I interviewed an amazing seventeen-year-old boy who wants to come and live here," Alice said. "He's perfect for the community. A very wise, old soul with a lot of talents. He can buy a trailer and move to Gypsyland next summer when he turns eighteen. Can we reserve a space for him now in case Gypsyland fills up?"

"If you say he is amazing, then I'll make an exception and he can join Team Creator. I normally only do this for family members, but we are looking for young, old soul men. As you know, women outnumber men around here."

Sarah smiled. "Thank you! He is going to be so excited."

John smiled. "No problem, and I want to see you dancing tonight."

John got up and walked away.

"Let's go help with the dishes and then do the sound chamber," Maddie said.

Alice got up. "Okay. I'm ready."

"What's the sound chamber?" Sarah asked.

"We'll show you," Maddie said.

They took their plastic plates and silverware and walked toward the cafeteria. The myriad of tables were about half-full, with people spread out into different groups.

Near the cafeteria, there were large plastic bins where people placed their dirty dishes and silverware. Each of the girls grabbed a full bin and carried it into the cafeteria. They found people in the back washing the dishes, and they joined them. After about twenty minutes of cleaning dishes, they headed out.

"Where's the sound chamber?" Sarah asked.

"It's over here. It's not far," Maddie said.

They approached a wooden building that was about thirty feet tall and about twenty feet wide. It was a bit of an odd shape and had no windows. Once they were inside, they could hear sounds. The building was well-insulated and kept the sound inside. They could hear gongs, crystal bowls, and a didgeridoo. Amazingly, inside, there was a large teepee that occupied the center of the building and stood thirty feet tall. This is from where the sounds were coming. The teepee was made out of wood and was insulated to keep in the sound. Around the teepee, on the ground floor, there were several small rooms.

"We need to wait until they finish, and then we can do the next one," Alice said.

"What is this place?" Sarah asked.

"It's a sound healing room," Alice said. "The sounds make your body vibrate, and it rebalances your energy. It takes about twenty minutes. It's dark inside, and you just meditate while they play the sounds. If you like it, you can volunteer to play the music."

"Also, these other rooms are where you can have bodywork done, which are, basically, healing massages," Maddie said.

"There is no bodywork on Saturday nights, but this place is busy all day on Sundays," Alice said. "I come all the time. If you do sound meditations and bodywork, it keeps your energy field balanced for optimum health."

"Very cool," Sarah said. "I can come here and do some healing for the locals. I can balance and clear their energy."

"Awesome," Alice said. "I want some of that, after watching you work."

"Me, too," Maddie added.

"No problem," Sarah said. "We can come for a massage, and then I will balance and clear both of you."

The sound stopped, and five people came out of the teepee. Each of the five people picked their shoes up off the floor, where they laid next to the teepee entrance. Several of the people greeted the girls as they put on their shoes and exited the building.

The girls took off their shoes, laid them next to the teepee entrance, and went inside. They found thirteen thin mattress pads pointing toward the center of the room. Each thin mattress was just large enough to hold one person. Each mattress had a pillow on the end that was closest to the center of the room. In the center of the room was a very large gong that was about five feet in diameter and four inches thick. Near the gong were several large crystal bowls. The mattresses appeared like spokes in a wheel that circled the musical instruments, which were the hub.

Alice talked to the people who were making the sounds and asked if they could do a session. Then she came back to tell Sarah and Maddie the situation.

"We have to wait for five minutes and then they will be ready to go again," Alice said.

"We should lie down and wait for them to begin," Maddie said.

They each found a mattress to lie on, next to each other. After they had laid down, Sarah looked at Alice. "What should I expect?"

"Your body will vibrate. Just relax and meditate. It's very comforting."

Sarah nodded and waited for the sounds.

After a short wait, the lights were dimmed until it was nearly pitch-black. They started with the crystal bowls, which hummed in beautiful tones. Then they added the gong, which made the entire room vibrate. The drummer beat the gong in a fast rhythm with two large padded drumsticks. Finally, someone with a didgeridoo walked around the room, playing, and moving the sound around. All three sounds intermingled and created a very soothing effect on the body. After twenty minutes, which seemed much longer, they stopped playing.

Sarah did not want to get up. She felt so relaxed that she wanted to stay. Alice and Maddie left her and went outside the teepee and put on their shoes. A few minutes later, Sarah came out.

"That was amazing!" Sarah said. "My body was vibrating."

"It's the teepee," Maddie said. "It makes the sound bounce off the walls."

"I want to try it naked," Alice said.

Sarah started laughing. "Why am I not surprised?"

Maddie started laughing. "Let's go dance."

As they exited the sound chamber building, they could hear the band playing off in the distance. It was already dark, but they could see their way from the lights that lit the path. All of the paths near the buildings had LED lights to make it easy to see their way.

Once they got close enough, they could see people dancing in front of the band. About half of the dinner crowd had left. People were dispersed throughout the area, sitting at the tables. The people who wanted to talk stayed further away from the band.

The band was loud, but not ostentatiously loud like a rock concert. The quality of the sound was pristine and enjoyable to the ear. The song they were currently playing was not really dance music, but people tried to dance to it. Many of the songs they played were not songs where you would normally see people dancing. John Randall liked Van Morrison's music from the 1980s, and many of those songs were played. Usually, the band would play at least two of Van's songs from the '80s. They were currently playing *Enlightenment*. It was stunningly beautiful to hear.

"That sound is amazing," Sarah said.

"They're good," Maddie commented.

"They sound better than most of the bands I listen to," Sarah said.

"We get this every Saturday night," Alice said.

They made their way to the dance floor, and all three of them started dancing together. It wasn't long after, when Mike and one of his friends joined them. They danced for about three songs and then took a break.

"Let's listen to the band from a distance," Alice said.

They all followed Alice to a section that was empty, toward the cafeteria, and sat down at a table.

"My body is still vibrating from the sound chamber," Sarah said.

"You guys went to the chamber tonight?" Mike asked.

"Yeah," Maddie replied.

"You should have invited us," Mike said.

"Next time, we'll look for you," Alice replied.

"I heard that they are working on adding lasers to the sound chamber," Tim, Mike's friend, said.

"Yeah, that's true," Alice said. "It's a technology from Atlantis for rejuvenation. We're supposed to get it sometime next year."

"Sarah, you need to go to John's lecture in the morning," Mike said. "He always speaks at ten a.m. on Sundays."

"Definitely," Alice said. "I always go."

"Me, too," Maddie and Tim added.

"Okay, where is it held?"

"Right here," Alice said. "He speaks from the stage."

"Afterward, we have brunch, and then put away the tables and chairs," Maddie added.

"I usually go for a run before and then get a bodywork massage," Mike said.

Sarah smiled. "I swear this place is heaven. Someone pinch me because I must be dreaming."

"I wouldn't want to live anywhere else," Maddie said.

"None of us would," Tim said. "Sarah's right. This is heaven."

"When's the next road trip?" Mike asked.

"In two weeks," Alice said. "We're going to Denver for a weekend."

"Can I go?" Sarah asked.

"You're in," Alice said. "Everyone in the youth movement is invited."

"What are we going to do in Denver?" Sarah asked.

"We're holding a two-day conference for young people who want to join Team Creator," Alice said. "We don't have an age limit, but we try to attract people in their youth. We get a lot of teenagers and people in their twenties and early thirties."

"So, we give lectures?" Sarah asked.

"Yeah, we have a schedule," Alice said. "The main speaker is John, but many people in the youth movement also speak. We also do a lot of one-on-one with visitors to answer their questions. That is what we will be doing."

Sarah got a bit nervous and looked at Alice. "Can I sit with you? I don't want to have to answer questions by myself. I could do it, but I'm such a newbie."

Alice smiled. "Sure, no worries. We can answer the questions together until you are comfortable."

"A lot of us pair up to answer questions. That's normal," Mike said.

"What kind of questions do you get?" Sarah asked.

"The gamut. Usually, they want to know what we believe in," Tim said.

"Which is?" Sarah said, looking at Tim.

"We believe that we are eternal souls having a human experience," Tim said, looking back at Sarah. "We believe that each soul is evolving and on a unique journey that is specific to that soul. For this reason, no two souls have the same journey, nor the same truth. What is true for one soul is not necessarily true for another.

"Judging another is nothing more than hubris and a lack of spiritual awareness. It is a lack of understanding of what life is about. God is perfection, and we are God, making us perfect. This underlying perfection negates the concept of right and wrong. Thus, there is no right and wrong; there is only experience. However, experiences have repercussions, or what many call karma.

"Experiences lead to other experiences. If you choose to have a negative experience, then that could lead to additional negative experiences. If you choose to have a positive experience, that could lead to additional positive experiences. This is why we live by God's virtues. They create positive experiences and bring us closer to our true self, which is perfect harmony.

"We believe that fear and the truth cannot coexist. The reason why is because our true self does not know fear. So, if we are experiencing fear, it is coming from the ego. However, if we are aligned and closely connected to our true self through our heart-center, then we should not experience fear. So, the higher we align, the more we shine!"

Tim paused. "That's enough for now. Once you start listening to John's lectures, you will catch on fast."

"I've read his books," Sarah said confidently. "I grasp what you are saying."

Tim smiled. "Excellent."

"One key belief that Tim did not mention," Mike said, "is that we live more from our heart than our head. The head cannot be trusted. You need to feel guidance from within to lead you. It's your soul, more than your brain, that has spiritual intelligence. The brain is a spiritual infant, or worse.

"Our consciousness has its own brain. This is why when people have NDEs, near- death experiences, or out-of-body experiences, they retain their intelligence. The soul is much more intelligent than the brain. That is where our wisdom resides."

"I understand," Sarah said. "That is what marginalizing the ego is all about. We have to allow the soul to lead us. That is our touchstone, our guide."

They all nodded.

"Good girl," Maddie said.

"Oh, I love this song," Alice said.

"You two go and dance," Sarah said to Alice and Maddie. "We'll stay and talk."

Alice smiled. "Okay, we'll be right back."

Alice and Maddie started skipping to the dance floor.

The band was playing a song from Death Cab For Cutie, *Little Wanderer*. It was a beautiful rendition.

You're my wanderer.

Little wanderer.

All across the sea.

"Mike, what do you believe?" Sarah asked.

"I believe that Christianity and most of the other religions are a big deception. Life is not about salvation. Jesus did not die on the cross for our salvation. He came to show us that we could be like him. He was an example to aspire toward. Yes, he was the son of God, but so are we. Life is about spiritual evolvement, but more than that, it is about achieving spiritual mastery. We are all trying to become ascended masters..."

"What is that?" Sarah interrupted.

"We exist today in the third dimension. The spiritual dimensions go much higher. Souls aspire to ascend to these higher dimensions. However, they can only be accessed by expanding our spiritual awareness. An ascended master is one who has reached these higher dimensions.

"In fact, until a soul has evolved sufficiently, they are stuck in the lower levels. These are immature souls, who must be guided by more advanced souls. An immature soul, or non-ascended master, automatically returns to these lower levels when their soul leaves their body at the end of this lifetime. However, an ascended master is free to go to the higher levels on their own. They become their own teacher."

"That's fascinating," Sarah said.

"It's also somewhat depressing," Tim said.

"Why?" Sarah asked.

"Because nearly everyone on this planet is not an ascended master," Mike said. "We are ascended masters in training. And if we fail, we have to do it again."

"The karmic wheel?" Sarah asked.

Mike nodded. "Exactly. We are stuck on the wheel, and most people are clueless of this fact. This is the big deception. No one is being told why we are here, which is to evolve through acts of love. You either learn the mastery of love, or you don't."

"So, eventually, we ascend to the higher dimensions?" Sarah asked.

"Yes. That's why we are here," Mike replied.

Alice and Maddie arrived back from dancing.

"That was fun," Alice said, sitting down.

"We've been talking about becoming an ascended master," Mike said.

Maddie rolled her eyes. "That's a big topic. Why can't we just have fun tonight?"

Mike smiled. "Sure, I think we were finished anyway."

Sarah looked at Mike, who returned her knowing look. They both knew that they would be talking more about it.

"Now's the time!" Alice said, looking at Sarah.

"What?" Sarah said.

"Let's go ask John why he did your compatibility with Mike," Alice replied.

Alice rose to her feet. "Come on."

Everyone followed her.

They found John and Julie, along with Sarah's parents, Tony and Teri, and Steve and Kate, all seated together.

All of the adults smiled and were happy to see Sarah and her friends.

"Are you having a good time, Sarah?" John asked. "Did you dance?"

Sarah smiled. "Yes, I did, and I'm having the time of my life. This is heaven."

"Are you coming tomorrow morning to my lecture?" John asked.

"Yeah, they told me not to miss it," Sarah said.

"We always come," Alice said to John.

"I can always count on the youth movement to attend. Thanks, guys."

"Don't mention it," Mike said. "If you take us on road trips, we'll be there for you."

John laughed.

"Sarah is already psyched about Denver in two weeks," Maddie said.

John looked at Sarah. "Excellent. So, you joined the youth movement?"

"The first day I was here, Alice took me to the youth movement trailer. I joined immediately."

"We have a question for you, John," Alice said.

"Sure, anything," John replied.

"Why did you do Mike and Sarah's compatibility?" Alice asked.

John hesitated. "Why do you ask?"

"I found it odd because I've never seen two people so closely compatible. The fact that you did the compatibility means that someone told you about it in advance."

John laughed at her intuitive hunch. "You're right, Alice. My guide, Joe, told me. He said those two are soul mates. So, I checked their compatibility."

Everyone was quiet. Tony and Teri glanced at each other. Mike and Sarah looked at each other.

"Well, it's all good," Maddie said. "They are already talking about ascended masters. They are like peas in a pod."

Sarah and Mike smiled, and everyone laughed.

* * * * *

The next morning, about fifty people gathered around the stage to listen to John's Sunday lecture. John stood in the center of the stage in front. He motioned for everyone to gather closer so that he did not have to use a microphone.

"Please come close to the front so that you can hear me," John said.

He waited for several people to move closer.

"Please stand if you want to volunteer to do the hand prayer," John said.

About twenty people stood. John covered his eyes with one hand and pointed at the crowd with his other. He moved his arm from side to side and then stopped. He opened his eyes to see who he was pointing toward.

"Ah, you're the lucky winner," John said.

They did this each Sunday morning. Sarah did not know what was going on, but everyone else did. The selected person came to the stage. She stood on the red X where John pointed. It was in the center of the stage, near the front. This is also where he stood to give the lecture. They recorded his Sunday lectures with a camera located a few feet in front of the stage and pointed toward the center.

"My name is Kristi, in case you didn't know. I'm a three of spades. A Taurus with Cancer rising, and my moon is in Aquarius. I'm fifteen years old and a seven lifepath."

She stuck out her thumb on her right hand. "Who do I serve? The ego or the soul? I serve the Creator, the universe, and my soul. I do not serve my ego. My thumb represents selfless service to humanity."

She stuck out her index finger on her right hand, leaving her thumb extended. "What example do I set? How am I perceived by others? Am I perceived the way that I want to be perceived? I choose to live a life that is an example for humankind."

She stuck out her middle finger on her right hand, while keeping her thumb and index finger extended. "The middle finger represents the sin of pride. Do I choose to be an egotist, narcissist, and hedonist? No, I choose to live a life of innocence, with humility and gratitude. I choose a life of giving, instead of taking."

She stuck out her ring finger on her right hand. Now all of her fingers were extended, except her pinky. "The ring finger represents treating others with unconditional love. This is where we use kindness, consideration, and compassion in our relationships with others. How we treat others is the golden rule."

She stuck out her pinky on her right hand. Now all of her fingers and thumb were extended. "The pinky is our commitment finger.

It is our allegiance, our intent, our objective, to live God's virtues. The pinky may be small, but it is the most important. We use the pinky swear to remain committed to our objective."

Kristi walked off the stage, down the stairs in the front. Everyone applauded. A few people whistled their appreciation.

"Well done," said John from the stage, where he stood by himself. "Before we get to my main topic, I want to talk about some of our core beliefs, since we have at least one newcomer in the crowd.

"We are eternal souls having a human experience. No one is living their first incarnation; in fact, most of us have lived hundreds or even thousands of incarnations. These incarnations all have the same objective, which is to evolve the soul.

"The soul evolves only one way, which is through the act of love. This is why we try to live God's virtues, which are all acts of love. Why is love so important? Because it is literally the core of who we are. Life is a long journey of understanding about love. Each lifetime adds a bit more knowledge. Eventually, we become enlightened with spiritual wisdom.

"Everyone is unique and on a unique journey. How they become enlightened is up to them. It is an individual experience. They choose their path. No two people have the same path, nor do two people have the same truth.

"While spirituality is an individual experience, we can help each other achieve our objectives. This is done through acts of love. Sharing our lives through intimacy, friendship, or community are all acts of love. This is our way of sharing God with each other.

"We can honor our journey and that of others through deep self-respect for the Creator and ourselves. It is through this deep self-respect that allows us to act in love. The more we act in love, the closer we get to our true selves. The hand prayer is one way of getting into alignment of living God's virtues.

"Be aware that when you are considerate to others, it is an act of love. When you are kind to others, it is an act of love. When you respect others, that is an act of love. When you are compassionate to others, it is an act of love. Actually, following any of God's virtues is an act of love."

John paused and scanned his audience.

"This brings me to today's topic, which is harmlessness. The term harmlessness encompasses kindness, compassion, and consideration. It's God's virtue of how we treat others. This is how we can honor everyone's path. We have our journey, which we can control, and they have their journey, which they can control. It's not our job to save anyone. After all, everyone is an eternal soul. They will figure it out. If not in this lifetime, then the next one. Your job is to figure out your way and stay out of everyone else's way.

"Everything happens for a reason. Moreover, every aspect of our lives was pre-planned and is predicated on our beliefs. Our beliefs are like magnets drawing us to experiences. That is why our lives are perfect. We are getting exactly what we believe.

"Most people do not accept this concept. Most people look at their lives as a series of random events. However, there is order to our lives. In fact, all of our potential experiences have already happened. Life is very much like a computer simulation that has already taken place. This is why randomness and God's plan for our lives are completely at odds with each other. Everything that is possible has already happened.

"Most people deny that life is perfect. This is where judgment comes from. This is where fear comes from. This is where addictions come from. When you do not live by God's virtues, you end up with experiences that most would consider negative. How can all of these negative experiences be perfect? Because that is what the soul has chosen to learn from. It may be negative, but it is still perfect. It is still the hand of God. It is still God's plan, and the ultimate outcome is positive.

"God's plan includes all possible outcomes. These are potential future timelines. We choose together, as a civilization, which timelines to go down. Within God's plan are the myriad of plans that each of us has made. What brings our plan to life is our beliefs, which are all pre-programmed. Our beliefs are not created after we're born, but *before*. We bring them with us from our soul. Some of our beliefs are hidden and need to be awakened, but the potential has been determined in advance.

"Once we realize that we are creating our own life through our pre-programmed beliefs, we can accept it. From that point of acceptance, we can learn to be harmless to ourselves and to society. We can forgive ourselves and anyone who has done us harm, and go forward with our lives, leaving the past behind. Moreover, no matter what we have created to this point in our lives, we can accept it with humility and gratitude. We can begin to understand that not only are our lives enough, they are exactly what we need."

John paused to emphasize his point.

"Once we get to this point of spiritual awareness, harmlessness becomes possible. We become aware that everyone's life is perfect, and then act in accordance with that realization. We come to the recognition that the world is divinely ordered. Once this recognition is real, we change from living by faith to living by *knowing*. This allows us to trust God's will, or what I like to call God's grand plan.

"Harmlessness is a state of being where we no longer identify with our egos. Instead of competing with others and forcing our will upon them, we allow others their freedom, their journey. Instead of competing, we act in service. We accept what is as perfection. We accept everything that happens as a blessing. This is how we create a frequency of love, a tone of love.

"Those who cannot accept what is as perfection are in denial of the divine. They are either denying the divine in themselves, or in others. The only blasphemy is the denial of the divine, which is the acceptance of the illusion of separation.

"Harmlessness occurs when there is a recognition that we are all one and in a state of cooperation, which allows everyone their sovereignty. It is recognizing that everyone is trying as hard as they can. By being harmless, we are loving others unconditionally and allowing them to live as they see fit. We become aware that the ego personalities that people reflect are an illusion, and the true self of each person is much more than apparent.

"As evolved souls, our job is to shine our light by setting an example of being harmless. That way, when people are looking for understanding, we can be there to help. It is the evolved harmless old soul who people will turn to. These are the people they will trust. Evolved souls carry an enormous amount of light that needs to be shared with the world. This is why newagers are also called lightworkers. The light that they work with does not come from a man-made light source, but is, instead, the essence of God. Most lightworkers simply project their light out to the world, but many of them are healers and work directly with this light.

"Many people struggle with their lives. Moreover, they do not feel enough love in their lives. From this absence of love, they are constantly looking to others for a shred of understanding. This is where harmlessness comes in.

"When we stand before someone without judgment, with only unconditional love, he or she can feel our support and compassion. This acknowledgment goes further when we are consistently harmless. By being harmless, we offer the kind of support and care that people can trust.

"We all need to be harmless to get along in a utopian society. Although we may not have a utopian society today, that does not mean we cannot aspire toward one. For instance, when the doorbell rings, and there stands a person in need, the harmless person responds in a positive way and does not inflict additional pain.

"Each of us has incredible opportunities to add love and light to this world. We constantly have opportunities to affect other people's lives in positive ways. Being harmless allows us to seize these opportunities. Being harmless allows people to live as they choose, not only the choices we agree with, but *all* of their choices. This is a radical idea in our current society in which the concepts of right and wrong are so highly valued. I am suggesting that we support *all* choices. Not just the choice to be a doctor, but the choice to be anything they choose."

John paused and looked at the camera that was recording the lecture.

"How many people are unhappy today because their family and friends withheld support for their choices? Choices such as which friends to have, which clothes to wear, which lifestyles to pursue. How many criminals started down the road to crime as angry teenagers because people refused to accept their choices? Is it their fault their anger and alienation led to criminal behavior?

"Maybe I am wrong on this point, but I believe I am a lot closer to the truth than the current condemnation of individuals. I know my ideas are not widely accepted. I also know the reason I incarnated was to shake people up. The coming civilization will be much closer to these ideas than the current prevailing beliefs.

"At the heart of harmlessness is unconditional love. We understand that each soul is perfect and does not need to do anything to achieve salvation. From this understanding, we are able to love each person without condition. Conditional love, the love that is prevalent in society today, is based on achievement and behavior. The belief in conditional love prevents people from being harmless.

"Here is an example of what I mean by harmlessness. A lady at work changes her hair length from long to short. Instead of allowing her to have the new hairstyle with little notice, people make a big thing of it. Those who like it smile and give her a compliment, whereas others grimace or snicker. Instead of being harmless, the co-workers are harmful. They cannot help themselves from judging her.

"People are so caught up in their false ego personalities that any change to their environment is perceived as a threat. To maintain their identities, they threaten others with emotional trauma if they dare to break from the norm. People are always on the lookout for violators to our societal norms.

"Ego causes people to harm each other constantly, not physically, but emotionally. As mentioned previously, instead of being harmless, most people are harmful. Why do people like to 'stick in the knife' with a verbal barb? And I am not just talking about saying it to the victim's face. I am talking about gossip, which is pervasive in society.

"Do we really think we can say something about someone else without ramifications? Every word we utter and every thought we think has ramifications and consequences. Not only that, but every word, every thought is recorded, and everyone has access to this record. Those people you talk about have access to your thoughts. Not in this life, of course, but after. Once this life is over, they will review their life prints in the Akashic records. Your thoughts will be in there.

"Look at the ramifications of gossip. Words have power, more than we perceive. When we talk about people in a negative way, we harm them. Did that sentence hit home? Do you not believe me? Do you think idle chat about other people is harmless? To the contrary, thought has power because thought is energy. Words are as real as physical force. Is that not what gossip is? A verbal attack? Words and thoughts have power. Think about it.

"People talk about each other because they identify with their own ego personalities. Most people think their ego personality is real, that their current personalities are their true identities. The fact is, the current personality is an illusion. It is only a temporary construct being used for this lifetime. Thus, the identities that people perceive as real are not real.

"To make an analogy, life is like a theatrical play. Everyone is playing a role, and that role is the personality. To get an idea of how this works, think of Al Pacino, the actor. You have probably seen him in numerous roles in several movies. However, if you met him on the street, would you know him? No. Instead, you would identify him with the personalities he has played, even though they were only roles.

"Our true self is spirit. Our true self is a compilation of the many incarnations and experiences we have had. When we shed the personality of this present life, our spirit appears. Our spirit identity is much different than our physical personality role. This is why we are more than we appear. A pauper has been a king, a king a pauper. A criminal has been a saint, a saint a criminal."

John looked at someone in the audience. "Do you know your role?" he asked. He looked at someone else. "Do you know yours?"

He waited while the audience pondered.

"Most people identify strongly with their personality because they believe it is real. From this belief, people are constantly defining their identity. Because people believe their identity is all they have, they feel a compulsion to constantly define themselves, as well as to defend the identity they have created.

"This compulsion is the source of harm because people are constantly defining themselves by comparing their identity with others. This is why people talk about other people and judge other people. People think they are real, and they feel compelled to define their reality.

"I call it a source of harm because it is the opposite of harmlessness. Instead of allowing and thus spreading love, people withhold love and spread judgment. When people identify with their personalities, they feel compelled to attack those who impinge on their identities. People create their own little worlds in order to define themselves, and then they defend them.

"Instead of being aware that life is a play, and we are all actors, people think their personality is real. From this belief, they spend all of their time defining their personalities. Instead of realizing that God is in charge of the destiny of this planet, they think they are in charge of their own little worlds. Thus, people subvert God's will by following their own ego will. In essence, people have lost touch with God, and they do not know how to be harmless.

"In today's culture, people believe that the pursuit of happiness is the only option. People live to satisfy their personal dreams and desires. From this perspective, they live for themselves. They follow *their* will to satisfy *their* needs.

"The pursuit of happiness is often a denial of God's will. Why? Because it often implies a lack of satisfaction and contentment with what God has provided. Today, most people believe happiness can be found through satisfying dreams and desires. This is what keeps people from being harmless. They are too preoccupied with chasing happiness and living by their desires to become harmless. Their ego is in charge."

John scanned the crowd, then he stared into the camera that was recording the lecture. Some people were watching it live on the Internet, and others would download it later. "Thank you, everyone. Until next week, this is John Randall."

Team Creator

Chapter Five

ON THE ROAD

Two weeks later, fifteen members of the youth movement, along with four adult chaperones and two cooks, hit the road for an event in Denver. They took three large motorhomes and two trucks. Both trucks were loaded with supplies, which consisted of food, water, and various sundries that teenagers and young adults could not live without.

The five vehicles drove close together in a convoy. They had cell phones and two-way radios to keep in contact and report any problems. After an eight-hour drive through central Colorado, they arrived at an RV park in Englewood, which was a short drive from the event. They had reservations for three RV hookup locations in the park.

They found their spots and got their water and electrical hookups situated. It was still early in the afternoon, and the weather was not too cold for an October day. Everyone found something to do. The two cooks who had come along began prepping for dinner. Some of the kids went exploring the area, others took out folding chairs and found a place to sit near the motorhomes. The rest of the kids stayed inside the motorhomes.

The four adults consisted of John and Julie Randall and two of their friends. They found a place to sit away from kids, who had the freedom to do what they wanted. From their experiences on previous trips, the kids knew to respect what Team Creator represented. They were here for a mission that, in many ways, could be considered sacred. John and the adults rode in the trucks, to allow the kids and young adults to bond and recognize that what they were doing was important. They were the next generation who would rebuild America into a new society.

John gave the kids their freedom, but he also demanded an allegiance to the Creator. These fifteen young adults were chosen to represent Team Creator. They were the faces and voices who would interact with the public. They were John's surrogates. Each of them was expected to be able to give public lectures about what Team Creator represented. In fact, many of them would be giving lectures tomorrow, at the weekend event.

Sarah, Alice, Maddie, and Mike were together in one of the motorhomes. They had become a close circle of friends since Sarah had arrived. Mike wanted to be with Sarah, and Maddie wanted to be with Alice, and Sarah wanted to be with Alice. The only solution was for all of them to hang out together, which they all enjoyed. Often Mike would bring one of his friends and make it a group of five.

"What are we going to do tomorrow?" Sarah asked the group.

"We get up early and go to the event," Maddie said.

"I know," Sarah said. "I meant at the event."

"We will set up some booths and find one to work in," Alice said. "We sit and answer questions from the visitors."

"If you want, you can attend some of the lectures," Maddie said. "The booths are pretty quiet during that time."

Sarah looked at Alice and Maddie. "Are you both going to have your own booth?"

"Why don't you and Mike share a booth together, and then Alice and I can share one together," Maddie said.

"Okay, but let's get two booths next to each other," Sarah urged.

Alice smiled. "Sure, we can do that."

On the Road - Chapter Five

* * * * *

The next morning, the group got up early and went to the convention center to set up their booths and test the sound system for the lectures. They had more than an hour before the doors opened. They were expecting at least 500 visitors. The entry price was only $5, which was used to help pay for renting the convention center. The fee would not cover the entire rental charge, but John wanted to keep it low, so that more people would attend.

Doors opened at 8 a.m., with the first lecture at 9 a.m. Team Creator sold various items at some of their booths. They sold John's books, DVDs and CDs of his lectures, custom jewelry, crystals, and artwork. Once the doors opened, customers headed for the booths to see what was for sale. The income they received helped pay for the cost of the trip. Usually, the door charge and sales would not cover the entire cost of the event. So, in effect, Team Creator subsidized the event.

About half of the booths sold something, and the other half were populated with members of the youth movement. They were there to answer questions about Team Creator. They each had colorful Team Creator signs on the walls behind their booths. This is where Sarah, Mike, Alice, and Maddie were seated. They were paired up in booths next to each other. They were close enough that they could talk to each other.

"It's almost nine," Alice said, looking at Sarah in the booth next to hers. "You should go find a seat to listen to John's lecture."

"Take Mike with you," Maddie said.

"Why?" Sarah asked, getting up.

"So that we don't have to babysit him," Alice said, with a smile.

Sarah rolled her eyes, knowing the real reason was that they had been playing matchmaker the entire trip. They just wanted Sarah and Mike to be together. Sarah thought she should just kiss Mike in front of them, so they could find something else to focus on.

Mike got up. "No problem, I'll go."

Sarah and Mike went into the lecture hall and found a place to sit. It was a large room, with a seating capacity of about 1,000 and it was about half full.

"John's going to talk about the meaning of life," Mike said. "I read the schedule."

"How long will he speak?" Sarah asked.

"About twenty minutes, and then he'll take questions."

"Can we ask questions?" Sarah asked.

"Sure, we're just part of the crowd."

Sarah nodded. "This is going to be cool."

"Yeah, a lot of these people have never heard metaphysical concepts. He changes a lot of lives, in a good way."

Sarah pointed out John, as he walked toward the stage.

John found his way to the stage and placed a cordless headset over his ear.

"Good morning, everyone. I'm John Randall. We have three lectures scheduled for you today. I always like to open the event with the meaning of life and some of the core beliefs that we hold at Team Creator."

John scanned the room and could see that the majority of people were under 30, although a significant portion were older than 30.

John put his right hand high over his head. "How many of you are new to the idea of Team Creator?"

About a quarter of the audience raised their hands.

"Okay, we have some new people who need to be educated. Team Creator is something that anyone can join. It's actually not an organization. You become a member of a group of like-minded people. It is actually a pact that you make with the Creator. You agree to live God's virtues, to expand the light on the planet.

"This is not something that is easy to do. Why? Because living God's virtues means that you have surrendered your ego to live in service to the Creator. This means that the ego must be marginalized and controlled, so that hedonism, narcissism, and egotism are non-existent in your life.

"It requires that you lead the life of someone in allegiance with the Creator. Your objective and commitment are for helping others and to augment God's grand plan. Your life is spent in service to humanity."

John paused and scanned the room.

"So, what is God's grand plan? It's to bring love to the planet. That is the objective, and that will be the outcome. In fact, most of you will be here to experience this outcome in your lifetime, at least the nascent beginning. However, in order for this outcome to be realized, the people of light must shine so brightly that darkness has nowhere to hide.

"You shine your light by living God's virtues. This allows you to spread the light and maintain a strong aura. Conversely, if you are angry, confrontational, argumentative, fearful, hedonistic, selfish, narcissistic, and many other unvirtuous traits, then you will not be spreading the light. Instead, you will be spreading disharmony, which is essentially spreading darkness.

"Now, we do not need to go to war with the dark. Nor do we need to go around pointing fingers at those in the dark. Instead, all we have to do is live God's virtues and be an example. This has the effect of spreading the light. Our auras become stronger and more influential, in a positive way. This influence is enough to change the world into a place of love. Our example is all that is needed."

John paused again to let that sink in.

"You see, all we have to do to spread light is to do acts of love. Love and light are two sides of the same coin. They are essentially the same. Acts of love are acts of light. The light is the energy of love, and this energy flows and moves throughout the world.

"Now, what are acts of love? A simple smile is an act of love. Forgiving someone is an act of love. Petting an animal is an act of love. Being considerate to another is an act of love. Being nice. Being friendly. Being compassionate. All of these are acts of love.

"Do you get it? We all know what God's virtues are, and when you live them with intent, they become acts of love. This is how you spread the light. It's very simple, but also very difficult.

"Why? Because of the perception of separation. The ego tricks us into believing that we are separate from the Creator and separate from each other. The ego wants to believe that we should focus on ourselves first. Reversing the order, so that the Creator comes first, does not feel natural. What feels natural is thinking about yourself first. This is the trick that traps us. The ego uses our buttons to find ways to make us focus on ourselves, and to ignore the Creator. This is the test of life. This is why we are here. This is literally the meaning of life, which is to figure out that we have been tricked by the ego, which isn't real.

"Now we come to the heart of the lecture. Why did we each come here to this planet? Why did we each incarnate? The answer is both simple and complex. The simple answer is that our soul has chosen this life for the soul's evolvement, and to learn what is true (the truth is always true) and what is false (what is not true is false). The complex answer is that everyone's evolvement is unique and personable only to them.

"The next question is, how does one evolve? You evolve by learning about love. Love is real and love is true. The ultimate lesson is to learn that the self is ultimately one with God, another truth we need to learn. This leads one to have self-respect for not just yourself, but also God, and everyone, and everything else. Again, a truth, that we need to learn. Out of self-respect, which we come to learn, leads to perpetual acts of love. In other words, the only acts that make sense, are acts of love. This is the wisdom we are all learning. This is the wisdom of truth. Meanwhile, we are stuck in the false ego, which keeps us from this wisdom of truth.

And its primary tool is the illusion of separation, which convinces us to focus on ourselves first.

"Do you see how simple it is to become enlightened? All you have to do is see through the ego's trick and become in service to the Creator. Oh, but it's not so simple. The ego is a like a powerful drug addiction that won't let go. This is why Christians call the sin of pride the deadliest sin. Christians almost get it right. What they get wrong is that they don't understand that they are one with God, and thus do not require salvation."

John paused and scanned the room to see if everyone was following him.

"There are a lot of dichotomies in the meaning of life. For instance, we are all one, and none of us are separate. However, at the same time that we are one, we each have unique paths of evolvement. We evolve together as a whole, but at the same time, we evolve independently.

"Each one of us, when we leave this lifetime, will move on to our next opportunity for individual soul growth. While we are living together on this planet, we are each independently evolving our soul. Our acts of love support one another and humanity, but ultimately, these acts impact our individual souls in unique ways.

"Everyone is at a particular level of soul evolvement. Not just everyone in this room, but every soul in all of existence. We use our incarnations to evolve. That is the meaning of this lifetime. All souls on this planet knew, in advance, the types of lessons they would encounter. They purposely exposed themselves to those potential experiences.

"When this lifetime ends, each soul will then determine their next experience. For the vast majority of souls, that will be another incarnation, in which the soul inhabits a foreign body in a foreign land.

"For those souls who are advanced enough, they will have achieved a level of freedom where they can come and go as they desire. They can choose which of the many dimensions of existence they want to learn from next. For, life is a continuous learning experience and one of evolvement.

"Achieving this advanced level of spiritual awareness is one of our highest goals and the reason we have exposed ourselves to this planet, which has so much conflict and pain. The Creator allows planets like Earth to exist because they offer incredible amounts of diversity that allow for substantial soul growth.

"This planet is so challenging that even advanced souls get caught up in its darkness. Less advanced souls need incredible courage to even come here. The odds are stacked against most who come here. Many souls end up living quiet lives of desperation. This is why depression is so rampant in this country. People know intuitively that life should be more than this. They can sense that something is wrong, and it leads to depression.

"When you join Team Creator, it is your job to share your joy. It is a virtue of God to have humility and gratitude. This gratitude should manifest in endless amounts of joy. Why? Because the Creator has not only given you eternal life, but the ability to evolve the soul. There are countless souls who would like to be alive at this time on this planet, but there is only enough room for a few billion of us. And of those few billion who are here, most of them live in poverty.

"We live in one of the most prosperous countries in the world. If any soul should have gratitude, it should be those living in the developed countries on this planet. We are literally the chosen ones. We get to help humanity to evolve, not only on this planet, but in the entire universe. What is happening here is reverberating throughout the cosmos.

"What is happening here right now, during our lifetime, is the culmination of thousands of years of evolvement. This planet, at one time, was a harmonious place, but that was nullified during the age of Atlantis. At the end of their civilization, they allowed pride and hedonism to become their meme. No longer was intuition and a connection to the Creator the overriding meme. This is the meme that we are bringing back. It's one of selflessness and oneness. It's a meme of humanity first and love as our highest value.

"This new meme requires a high degree of intuition. People must be led from within. This requires a connection to Source. When you begin to live by God's virtues, this connection will become palpable and knowable. Your spiritual strength will increase until you become a powerful being. At that time, no one will be able to tell you what to believe because you will know for yourself what is true.

"What I am telling you has been hidden from humanity for thousands of years. This knowledge is being released at this time because God's grand plan is now to push out the darkness with light. Each one of you has the opportunity to spread the light, and usher in a new humanity.

"If you join Team Creator, you can be a member of the team that is helping to usher in this new humanity. You can help to spread light across the planet, and at the same time, you can get closer to your own soul, and closer to your true self. It is something I highly recommend if you feel an affinity to the Creator."

John paused and scanned the audience.

"Okay, who has questions? We have a microphone down here in the front."

John pointed at the microphone, which was attached to a microphone stand. Soon, several people were walking toward the microphone and forming a line.

"I have a question about karma," a young adult male said. "Are we all accumulating karma, both positive and negative? And can we live a bad life and go backward in our soul's evolvement?"

John looked out at the crowd. "A very intriguing question. One that I have also asked. The question really is, do my actions have ramifications? And the answer is clearly, yes. So, karma is real. How we live our lives matters, and it will impact our future lives. Moreover, it matters to humanity's future, and can impact the future lives of others.

"We are each on a journey of evolvement, and if we make bad choices, they can delay our goal. The good news is that everyone ends up at the same destination, which is enlightenment. So, even if it takes us fifty lifetimes to learn a lesson, while it takes someone else only five lifetimes, it is all arbitrary. The end result is the same. Life is perfection. I repeat. Life is perfection. Why? Because the Creator only knows perfection.

"This is something of a paradox. For instance, isn't it better to always make good choices? The answer is actually, no. Why? Because who decides what is a good choice or a bad choice? Life is more complicated than we can perceive. In fact, all of life is perfection, because that is the only existence that the Creator knows. For this reason, there is no right and no wrong. This is one of the most difficult concepts to grasp on your journey to enlightenment, and one that young souls tend to deny vehemently.

"So, to answer your question, can you go backward by accumulating bad karma? The answer is, yes, but that doesn't mean that it is wrong. You can spin your wheels and live many lives with very slow or negative progress. However, eventually, you will get it right. Remember, you are an eternal being, so time does not matter. Also, judgment does not exist. No one is going to be upset that you failed in your objective for this lifetime. That is, no one except, possibly, yourself."

John smiled mischievously, knowing his last response would keep people thinking about this question.

"Who's next?" John asked.

A young lady approached the microphone. "My question is about suicide. Is it acceptable, from the Creator's viewpoint?"

"Oh, I like these questions today. Another paradox question. When you find paradoxes, you are always getting close to the truth. The paradox is that, while there is no right or wrong, and no judgment, suicide is never a good choice. In fact, suicide is probably the least acceptable choice by the Creator.

"The reason why is because incarnations are amazing gifts. Not everyone gets to come to this planet. And those who do come, plan their lives carefully in advance. When someone commits suicide, it impacts all of those plans. Not only that, but it impacts additional future lives that have already been planned out. All of that planning goes poof. Thus, there can be huge ramifications, and the Creator can get a little bit prickly. If you want to get the Creator's attention, suicide a few times. Trust me, it won't be a pleasant outcome.

"Like everything else, the context and details of the situation come into play on the outcome of suicide. If you are tormented by mental health issues or are dying from a disease, then the outcome could have fewer ramifications. However, if you don't have a good excuse, the ramifications can be harsh.

"One thing to consider about suicide is that, if you use it to avoid a lesson, that lesson could increase in severity by a factor of two or more. Let me give you an analogy. Let's say that you are learning about gratitude and humility, but you commit suicide because you are depressed and not happy with your life. Those lessons will now become much more difficult. And if you suicide again, they become even more difficult. It's simply never a good idea to suicide. Stick it out, if at all possible. Don't think it will be better, once you get out of this body. You will quickly be back in another body, and probably in an even more difficult situation. You will just make matters worse.

"Okay, next question," John said.

"How is the darkness on the planet pushed out?" asked a young man. "How do we make evil go away?"

John smiled. "That is exactly the purpose of being a member of Team Creator. We are all lightworkers who are spreading the light. By spreading the light, we are spreading it all over the planet. This expansion of light increases the amount of love that is felt and decreases the amount of darkness and evil on the planet. In essence, we are squeezing them out.

"This squeeze would also happen automatically if we weren't trying to do it consciously and proactively as Team Creator. The reason why is because more and more people are feeling the new light energy on the planet. The flow of love is becoming much more natural to people than the flow of hate. This change began intensifying in the 1960s, and today it is manifesting on a global scale.

"Love and light are the same energy. As that energy spreads, it has the effect of pushing out the darkness. This is our role if we choose to accept it: to spread this energy. If you want to fight evil, if you want to fight darkness, then spread love. You can do this by spreading the light and being a member of Team Creator.

"However, even if you do not join, there is no reason to feel guilty, because the planet, itself, is evolving to the point where darkness will no longer be allowed. This is going to happen, one way or the other. The future of this civilization is love and light. The darkness will not be around much longer. We, at Team Creator, are just trying to speed up the process."

John pointed at the next questioner, an older woman.

"If we are all connected, doesn't that make us connected to God? And, isn't there just one consciousness, which is the consciousness of the Creator?"

John smiled and looked at the lady. "I like to call this the new meme of humanity, although it hasn't caught on yet on a global scale. In the near term, I think that it will, because it's true. We are all one. There is no separation between us and the Creator. This will be proven by scientists in the future, but until then, we have to discover it for ourselves.

"There are some scientists today working on this question, such as Rupert Sheldrake and Bruce Lipton. But by and large, it is still ignored by the scientific community. Some of the work on quantum theory delves into this topic, but they have not yet connected the dots to a proven theory.

"The potential of humans is nearly limitless because of our connection to Source. This is how Jesus and other spiritual adepts were able to perform miracles. We all have this connection to Source. It is also what connects us together.

"Today, there are millions of people who are tapping into this connection to obtain esoteric abilities that many people consider impossible. They are doing this by accessing the fourth dimension. The number of people who have esoteric abilities today is multiples of what it was a few decades ago. In another decade, nearly everyone will have these abilities. Perhaps, the two most ubiquitous abilities that will appear will be heightened intuition and telepathy.

"This connection to Source is becoming pervasive. And once you recognize it, spreading the light becomes second nature. Living God's virtues is how you want to live, because it not only feels right, but it becomes your personal truth. An awakening is happening right now on the planet, and that awakening is about this new meme. The ultimate outcome is peace on earth and a unity consciousness, in which everyone is aware of this meme, that we are all one consciousness, which we share with the Creator."

John paused and scanned the audience to see if this resonated. "Okay, last question."

"How do you know all this?" asked a young lady.

John sighed. "I've answered this question so many times, it's getting boring. For those in the crowd who have heard this before, bear with me. I'm a fifth-level old soul, priest-scholar. Now, what does that mean? I'm going to give you the short answer, but if you want to learn more, do some research on the Michael Teachings. It's fantastic information about the reincarnation cycle.

"There are seven soul types: king, priest, scholar, warrior, sage, artisan, and server. There are five soul stages: infant, baby, young, mature, and old. Everyone has either a single soul type, or a combination of two types. I'm a combination priest-scholar.

"There are seven levels in each soul stage. Thus, there are thirty-five levels that we must traverse, with each level providing a series of lessons. The old soul stage is the last one. This means that I am on level thirty-three. That is way up high on the continuum. I only have two more to go to complete my cycle. What's interesting about the thirty-third level is that it is the last one before you go into quiet time. The last two levels are generally spent getting close to the Creator, with much less social interaction.

"So, being a fifth-level old soul gives me a high degree of receptivity to spiritual information, plus the ability to share what I know. Then, being a priest-scholar, this gives me even more receptivity. The combination makes me wise and lucid, with regard to spiritual questions.

"An astrological chart defines your personality traits, but your soul type, soul stage, and soul level give much more information about who you currently are. I would much rather have this information about someone than their astrology, although I would like to have both."

John paused and scanned the crowd. "Okay, that's it. There will be another lecture in about an hour. Thank you for coming."

People started filing out of the room.

"Let's go answer questions," Sarah said.

"Sure," Mike replied.

They got up and made their way to their booth. There were at least a hundred people walking around near the booths. As soon as Sarah and Mike found their seats, someone approached them.

"What's the difference between Team Creator and being a Christian?" asked a young man.

On the Road - Chapter Five

Sarah looked at Mike, informing him that this was his question to answer. Then she glanced at Alice and Maddie next door, who were both busy talking to other visitors.

"Were you just at the lecture?" Mike asked.

"Yeah," replied the teenager.

"Did it resonate with you?" Mike asked.

"Yeah, I think so. I just have questions."

Mike smiled. "Cool. We can help. Team Creator is very similar to Christian doctrine and values. The biggest difference is the concept of being one with the Creator. Christians believe they are separate from God, and that their salvation is dependent on God's mercy."

"What do you believe?" Sarah asked the young man.

"I think oneness makes sense. I've always had a problem with the concept of God's judgment. I don't think God uses fear to entice us to follow him."

"Me, too," Sarah replied. "God is love. I know that God loves me unconditionally."

"What about reincarnation?" Mike asked. "Did you like what John said at the end?"

"Yeah, that was pretty cool. I've always believed in it. I have a friend who remembered a past life when he was younger, but those memories have faded."

"Awesome," Mike said. "Those are the two biggest differences from Christianity. Oneness and reincarnation. Once you get over those hurdles, we are basically on the same page. We believe that acts of love are the way to live. That was Jesus' message."

"There are a few other differences," Sarah said. "We do not believe in materialism or living ostentatiously. Instead, we prefer a more simple lifestyle, with a focus on service. We believe that selfless service to humanity is the best way to serve the Creator's grand plan. Also, we believe that all of life, all of humanity, are part of our extended family."

"I'm not a materialist, but I am a Christian," the young man said. "I don't think those are correlated."

Sarah smiled. "But you have to agree that many Christians do live affluent, materialist lifestyles."

The young man laughed. "Sure, but do you think God judges affluence?"

"No, there is no judgment," Mike chimed in. "Our preference for simplicity is in alignment with our belief in oneness. We think that God wants to bring humanity together, and the best way to do that is through selfless service and a simple lifestyle."

The young man nodded. "I get it."

"Here's our card," Sarah handed the young man a youth movement card. "It includes our website. You can ask questions or just read the blog. We're called The Youth Movement. We're trying to inform the youth of the world."

"I'll check it out, thanks," replied the young man, as he walked away.

"That wasn't too bad," Sarah said, after the boy was gone.

"We're a good team," Mike said.

Sarah smiled.

"How was the lecture?" Maddie asked.

"It was great," Sarah said. "I'm going to the next one."

"That's fine," Maddie replied. "We can handle anyone with questions during the lectures. It gets pretty quiet out here."

"How many lectures do you think it will take before I get bored?" Sarah asked.

Maddie laughed. "It depends on how fast you learn. Perhaps ten, maybe twenty."

"No, she's hungry for knowledge," Alice said. "More than twenty."

"She can ask Harper," Maddie said.

"Yeah! Great idea," Alice said. "I'll set up a reading. I think you and Mike should go together and get confirmation about what John Randall told you."

"Who's Harper?" Sarah said.

"She's our resident psychic. She is fantastic at doing readings," Alice said.

"You mean, like our future?" Sarah said.

Alice laughed. "Sometimes I forget that you're sixteen."

"She can tell you all kinds of stuff about your life and past lives," Maddie said. "Do you want to know?"

"Sure, that would be helpful," Sarah said with eagerness. "I would like to know what I am on this planet to do."

"Cool, I'll set it up," Alice said. "Mike, are you in?"

"Yeah, sure. I've never had a reading from Harper. It will be fun."

Mike and Sarah looked at each other, not knowing what they were about to experience.

Team Creator

Chapter Six

HARPER

Harper lived in one of the twelve houses that circled the main buildings. She lived in house number seven with her daughter. On most days, she did a single reading. She preferred to do one reading a day so that the information had more clarity. Harper was both a mystic and a psychic, as well as an energy healer. These were not her only talents and skills, but the ones on which she chose to focus. Often, she could be found at the healing center, where her third eye and psychic ability helped to diagnose patients' ailments.

Harper was over fifty, but no one knew her exact age, or even her birthday. She was very secretive and would not let anyone know her first name. It was kept a secret because of her respect for numerology. A person's name and birth date convert into five numbers. These numbers can tell you a lot about someone. Harper preferred that she remain a mystery.

She was one of the most respected members of Team Creator. John and Julie always included her in important meetings and listened carefully to her counsel. It was believed that Harper was either a seventh-level old soul, an ascended master who had incarnated, or perhaps, an alien walk-in. No one knew, and she wasn't saying. This was part of her mystery.

As Sarah and Mike approached Harper's house, they were nervous. They didn't know what to expect, but they had a deep respect for Harper's reputation. They expected to be told something about their future, and perhaps about their future together.

They knocked on the door and waited.

Harper smiled after she opened the door. "Come in. I've been expecting you."

Sarah and Mike walked in. They could tell by Harper's demeanor that she was a very strong woman. If the devil appeared in the room, they doubted if Harper would run. More likely, it would be the devil that would be leaving, as an uninvited guest. She was not someone to cross. She had an unusual disposition of both unconditional love and toughness, mixed with incredible spiritual strength. She was someone who would not allow the corruption of spirit in her presence. In some ways, she had the fighting strength of Archangel Michael, who, according to the Bible, led God's army against Satan. If there was such a thing as a soldier of God, she embodied it.

Sarah and Mike scanned Harper's living room. It was full of crystals and beautiful drawings by her granddaughter.

"Follow me," Harper said. "I have a special room where I do my readings."

Harper walked to the back of the house and entered a room. Inside were more crystals, including a huge amethyst cathedral that must have weighed three hundred pounds. She also had a large rose quartz obelisk that was sitting on a pedestal and reached more than halfway to the ceiling. There was incense burning, with the smell of sage. The house had wooden floors, but there was a carpet in the center of the room. Harper sat down behind a desk and motioned for Sarah and Mike to sit across from her on a sofa.

Harper picked up a small recording device that was on her desk and turned it on. "This will record our conversation, and I will email it to you after we are finished today. You are going to want to listen to it at least once, and I recommend that you save it for a future listening."

Harper paused. "Oh my," she said, somewhat startled, as she placed the recording device back down on her desk. "We have a powerful one with us today."

Sarah and Mike were still a bit apprehensive because of Harper's strength of demeanor.

Harper laughed. "Relax. You two are blessed more than you know. The powerful one is one of your guides. I'm going to close my eyes and let him talk to me for a few minutes. Then we can get on with the reading."

Sarah and Mike both nodded.

Harper closed her eyes. After a few minutes, she opened them. "You two have not kissed yet, have you?"

Sarah blushed. "No."

"But you both want to. Is that correct?"

Sarah looked at Mike. "I think so."

"No, that's not good enough," Harper said. "I need to know if you both want to kiss each other because your guide is giving me an odd request."

"I do," Mike said without hesitation. "I have since the moment I laid eyes on her."

"Me, too," Sarah said. "I'm sure."

Harper smiled. "Indeed."

Harper got up. "Come with me then."

Harper walked to another room and opened the door. "This is my daughter's room. She won't mind if you use it. You have ten minutes to make out. You can lie on the bed if you want. Come and find me when you are done."

Harper turned and went back to her reading room.

After about ten minutes, the two came back to the reading room, both beaming.

"I see that it went well," Harper said, smiling.

"Yeah, I don't know what we were waiting for," Sarah said.

"One of your guides said that it was important for you to bond before the reading. You are soul mates, but you are also twin souls. You will never part again in this lifetime. A very powerful connection exists between you two."

Harper paused to let it sink in. "That's probably why you had not kissed, yet. You both knew it was coming, and that there was no rush. The attraction between you two is powerful. Nothing is going to keep you apart. I would suggest that you both tell your parents that you have met your soul mate and that you know who you are going to spend the rest of your life with. Tell them you have found your twin soul, and that you have no doubts. They will understand."

Harper paused again.

Both Sarah and Mike knew there was something between them, but this was still stunning information. Both stared at Harper, soaking in the information.

"You can hold hands if you want," Harper said.

Sarah moved her hand close to Mike's and he grasped it.

"Wow," Harper said. "That was just the warm-up. We haven't even started the reading. In Sarah's past lives, she has been a priestess of a noble order. A queen. A princess. These are titles that she has held before, and some, on more than one occasion. She is practically nobility. In this life, however, she has come to be a healer and hide her nobility. However, her children will help change the world. You will have five children, and all of them will be highly evolved souls, with important missions to accomplish. They will bear your spark of nobility. We cannot do readings for each child today, but if you come back, we can do that.

"It is quite uncommon for twin souls to incarnate together. This is the first time that you two have done it. So, this is your first incarnation together. However, you are very similar souls, with similar pasts. Mike has been a high priest and a king in past lives. In this life, Mike is going to have a successful business, which will be used to fund both Team Creator and your children's ambitions. This business is going to be part of the drone industry. You are going to work with Sarah's uncle, who will help you with the software.

"Your expertise is going to be the designer of drones that can fly both above water and underwater. Your success will be based on inventions that you have not yet designed. You will create unique designs for futuristic drones. These designs will come from your higher self and are, in fact, similar to drones in other planetary systems. When you draw them, people will wonder where your ideas come from. They will come from within."

"That's amazing," Mike said. "I've already drawn a few drones, but I've never thought of designing one. I suppose I could."

"You will," Harper said.

"He's an amazing artist," Sarah said.

"I know," Harper said. "As good as my granddaughter. All of the pictures you saw in the living room are by her."

"They're beautiful," Sarah said.

Harper smiled. "I'll tell her you said so. Now, we need to get to the important stuff. If your lives are going to accomplish your goals, you need to know yourself."

Harper got up and went to a bookcase and removed a book. She sat back down and opened the book to a particular page.

"You are both an eight of diamonds in this lifetime." Harper smiled. "Isn't it interesting that twin souls came in with the same card? I guess you both knew that you were going to be similar, so why fight it? Why not embrace your similarities? Thus, you decided to be the same card."

"We decided?" Sarah said.

"Oh, yes, my dear," Harper replied. "We all choose who we are going to be. This is the life that you picked in advance. And your children will pick you, not the other way around."

Harper paused, and Sarah and Mike got the message not to interrupt her again unless they had a good question.

"All eights are hard workers and have perfectionist tendencies. You like your life to have a solid foundation and the ability to impact your surroundings. This inevitably leads you to wield power in some form or another. Your desire to create stability in your life can lead you to somewhat dominate your environment. However, you do this in a stealthy way so that people are not aware of your manipulation. You can even fool yourself of your objectives.

"This desire for stability will lead you to attract other powerful people into your life. These are people who can help you build and maintain your foundation. In most cases, this leads to a successful life for an eight, and especially for an eight of diamonds.

"The eight of diamonds has the ability to achieve their desires. In fact, most souls who chose to be an eight of diamonds do so for the specific reason of achieving something of significance. Your friends will be chosen for the specific purpose of supporting your foundation and ambitions.

"It is quite normal for an eight of diamonds to be held in high esteem. This occurs from your meticulous quest to build a life with no fragility. It has to be a solid foundation, or else it won't do.

"Your desire to control your environment turns you into a leader who is not comfortable being told what to do. This makes you a strong person, but also an independent person. This can be your weakness if you try to push others around, or try to push each other around. It will be difficult for you to trust others and to trust each other. However, you need to balance your need for control, with your need for harmony and joy. The more you seek control, the more harmony and joy will be endangered.

"Control what you can, but don't go too far. Allow others their sovereign right to exist. The hand prayer can help you with this. I recommend that you both say it at least once a day, and twice preferably, until it is firmly embedded into your consciousness. And don't let the prayer just be words. When you say that you are going to be considerate, kind, and compassionate, mean it and live it."

Harper paused. "Okay, Let's do Sarah's astrology and numerology. Then we'll do Mike's."

Harper got up and went to the bookshelf and exchanged books. She sat back down and turned to a specific page. "You have a twenty-seven, nine lifepath. This means if you add up all of the digits on your birth date, you will get twenty-seven. When you break down twenty-seven into a single digit, you get nine.

"Your lifepath is a combination of these three numbers, two, seven, and nine. You need to learn numerology and the energy of each of these numbers. Our lifepath is our chosen direction, and how we will accomplish our goals. For you, your goals will be accomplished through these numbers.

"Nine is integrity and wisdom. It is also leadership, but the core is really about integrity and wisdom. The seven is trust and openness. It is also spirituality, but the core is trust and openness. The two is cooperation and balance. This balance for you will be between living in this physical world of the third dimension and the spiritual side of life, which is within.

"When you combine these, it tells you your potential lessons in this lifetime. You need to cooperate with others through integrity and trust. If you don't, then these lessons will manifest. If you do, then the next lesson of openness and balance will arise, and you will be tested again. Ultimately, your success at manifesting trust will allow openness and balance to flourish.

"Conversely, if you are not in integrity, your wisdom will wither, and a lack of trust will prevent cooperation. Now, we don't want that, so you need to learn how to trust people and create a high degree of cooperation."

Harper paused to see if Sarah was listening carefully.

"Got it."

"Good," Harper replied. "Now, for all twenty-seven, nines, their ultimate lesson is to learn how to trust the heart. The heart is where wisdom resides. It is the key that unlocks your mastery.

It leads to trust, and it leads to cooperation. Then you are ready to open your heart to others and balance your life between this dimension and the higher dimensions. Thereby living closer to your soul."

Harper closed the book and opened her laptop lid. She pressed a few keystrokes and read from the screen. Then she turned to Sarah.

"You are a Scorpio, with Pisces rising, and your moon is in Taurus. This is a very powerful horoscope. As a Scorpio, you have incredibly deep emotions. Your quiet demeanor tends to hide these emotions well, but under the surface, you are a powerhouse of emotion. You also have a keen feel for life and death. This helps you with your healing abilities. You can look death in the eye and bring someone back to life.

"As a Pisces rising, the world sees you as someone who is generous and kind. However, they don't notice how sensitive you are and how you feel every word that is directed your way. You also have huge sympathy for others, including animals, and even nature itself. Others may notice your creativity, which is often on display.

"Your Taurus moon makes you sensuous and attractive to others. It also makes you a family person who loves spending time at home. If you are not at home, then you are probably thinking about it."

Harper paused.

"When I give a reading, I do not always tell people about their card, numerology, and astrology. However, this is what your guides told me that you needed today. They want both of you to learn about yourselves so that you can advance quickly into mastery.

"Both of you are here to give back to humanity in significant ways, and your children are going to impact humanity much more than you expect. Your job is to grow swiftly as individuals so that you can raise your children to be the magnificent souls that they are destined to become."

Harper - Chapter Six

Harper paused again and looked at Sarah.

"I know that you are young, but the Creator is asking that you grow up quickly. You are now part of the youth movement. You are soon going to be asked to do more than that. I know you can handle it, but over the next few weeks and months, please replay this reading and do some research on these subjects."

"Why is it so important that we know about ourselves?" Sarah asked.

Harper smiled. "That's not an easy one to answer. I usually leave the big philosophical questions to John, but I'll give you the short answer. Everyone, or nearly everyone on this planet, is trying to achieve something spiritually. This goal or objective is usually hidden, or at least partially hidden. Our job is to uncover it and achieve our life's lesson.

"Most people are completely oblivious to their life's lesson. This is mainly due to the fact that they do not know themselves. Thus, if you want to achieve your life's lesson, the best starting point is to know yourself. Does that make sense?"

Sarah nodded. "Yes."

"Do you know your life's lesson?" Mike asked Harper.

"I'm not sure if we have time for that. We need to focus on you two," Harper replied.

"How about the short answer?" Mike asked.

Harper rolled her eyes. "Okay. I'm not really here to learn lessons in this lifetime. I came as a volunteer. A call went out to the universe for advanced souls to volunteer to incarnate on Terra, that's Earth's real name. This call was urgent and of extreme importance.

"The planet was on the verge of destroying itself, and unless enough evolved souls incarnated in the twentieth and early twenty-first century, it wouldn't make it. This destruction almost happened, but the gathering of evolved souls prevented it. I'm part of that gathering, as are you.

"Now that we have prevented the destruction, a wonderful thing has happened. This is the secondary reason I incarnated. The planet has been ascending to a higher vibration because of the gathering of so many evolved souls. This makes it possible for humans to ascend, which is my new goal."

"How do humans ascend?" Sarah asked.

"That's another question that requires a long answer. The short answer is that I plan to vibrate off the planet and move to the New Earth, which is in the 5th dimension. Anyone who can do this will become an ascended master."

"I've heard about ascension," Mike said. "It's all over the Internet. Many people are trying to do it, but there is no proof anyone has succeeded. I'm not sure it's possible."

"It's possible, just not easy," Harper said. "If it was easy, I wouldn't be here. However, soon there will be peace on earth, and the vibration of the planet will increase even higher. There will be opportunities to ascend in the future."

Harper got up and went to the bookcase. "Okay, let's finish. It's time for Mike's reading."

Chapter Seven

DISCLOSURE

The next day Sarah and Alice went inside the youth movement trailer after their morning shift at the healing center. When they walked to the back, where they liked to sit, they found Maddie.

"Oh my God!" Maddie exclaimed. "Did you hear?"

"Hear what?" Alice said, as she sat down in the cubicle next to Maddie.

Maddie pointed at her screen. "Check this out!"

Alice moved to where she could see the screen.

"Holy crap," Alice said, in a shocked voice.

"What?" Sarah said, moving closer to Maddie's screen.

"Disclosure. They're finally telling the world that aliens are real!" Alice said in a stunned voice.

"Yeah, I've been reading about it," Maddie replied. "It's full blown. They're releasing everything, even a list of all the aliens who have ever visited. It's a long list. This is blowing people's minds."

"What about their spirituality?" Sarah asked. "Have they released what the aliens believe about God?"

"Oh yeah," Maddie replied. "There is an entire section on their spirituality. They know the truth that we are all one, and all connected. Their beliefs are just like ours at Team Creator. They know about reincarnation. Why wouldn't they? They are more evolved."

"This is the beginning of the new meme," Alice said. "The world is now going to change into a peaceful place, where love and humanity thrive. There will be no more wars, no more violence."

"Religions are toast after this," Maddie said.

"That's for sure," Sarah added.

"They are also releasing new technology that is amazing," Maddie said. "They have self-contained energy sources that last for years. They can be used to power transportation vehicles, homes, even communities. These new energy sources can be used to purify water efficiently, even salt water. The combination of cheap power and cheap clean water will make food production easy. We can use these new power sources here."

"This changes everything," Alice said. "It's a new world."

"This is what John has been writing about," Sarah said. "It's why he created Team Creator. He has been preparing for the truth to be released, and that day has arrived. I guess the world is ready to accept it. The illusion of separation is now exposed. The reality of reincarnation has been revealed. Our eternalness is no longer a secret."

"Yes, the truth has been released," Alice replied, "but that doesn't mean everyone will believe it."

"Yeah, a lot of people will consider the aliens to be the devil, and will deny all of it," Maddie said.

"Some will be in denial," Alice said, "but over time, humanity will come to accept the truth. It's our job to help humanity to understand. After all, we are the old souls. We're the ones who already know."

Sarah and Maddie nodded.

"Peace on earth is now within our reach," Alice said. "It's time to close the deal."

They were all quiet for a moment, contemplating how their lives had just changed.

Maddie sighed. "The youth movement is more important now than before. We have to get the word out."

Sarah smiled. "Count me in."

* * * * *

A couple of weeks later, a television crew came to Team Creator to interview John Randall. They wanted to talk about the fall of religions from the recent disclosure.

After the crew set up their lights and camera, John sat down to do a one-on-one interview.

"You are a bit of a prophet," the interviewer began. "You have been writing about the coming end of religions for twenty years. How did you know it was coming?"

"The truth can only be withheld for so long," John said. "At some point, it had to emerge in the mainstream. I have known the truth for a long time, as have millions of others. I simply wrote what I knew. I was confident that the truth would be released during my lifetime."

"What truth are you referring to?"

"That we are one with God and connected to one another energetically and consciously. That there is no separation between us. Any separation that we perceive is an illusion. All of life is connected consciously, energetically. This was part of the disclosure, but if you do some research, you will see that people have been writing about this for quite some time.

"Most people think that their consciousness is self-contained and that this makes them separate from everything else. People are not aware that their consciousness is not self-contained. In fact, it is literally entwined with everything around them. Our consciousness is not inside our bodies; instead, it surrounds our bodies. It then entwines with everything around us, which is part of an all-encompassing consciousness that is alive."

John paused and waited for a reply.

"So, the air is alive? This room is alive? How is that possible?" the interviewer asked skeptically.

"Because it is the consciousness of the Creator. We are all inside of this consciousness, and nothing exists outside of it. Some people call it the mass consciousness. This is the truth that has been withheld.

"Our soul is conscious energy. Ironically, this is something that many people accept as truth. However, what most people do not grasp is that our soul exists within the Creator's consciousness, which is also energy. This creates a pervasive consciousness that we all share. This makes us one with each other, and one with the Creator. Like I said, there is no separation."

"So, the air that separates us is simply interconnected consciousness?" the interviewer asked, skeptically.

John nodded. "Yes, and it's not just air that has consciousness. Everything you see in this room is alive with consciousness. This is how telekinesis works. Some people can move objects with their minds, and that is how they can do it. This is also how telepathy works. When you think of someone, your thoughts pass through this interconnected consciousness. What you are doing is using the Creator's consciousness as a connected network. It's much like the Internet, only it's always on, and much more powerful."

The interviewer let out a long breath. "This is blowing my mind. It's very difficult to get my head around it."

"That's your ego," John Replied. "Your ego wants to hang on to its identity. Once you grasp that you are not self-contained, the ego begins to lose its stranglehold, its identity."

"What do you mean?"

"The ego's role is to create an identity so that we can learn lessons in a state of amnesia. We have to forget who we are, which is God, in order to learn these lessons. And the ego will do everything in its power to hold on to this identity, because once it is exposed as a false identity, it loses its reason to exist.

"When you think you are on your own and self-contained, your ego plays a prominent role in your choices. The ego primarily uses fear to control our behavior, and the irony is that fear is often only an idea, and isn't real. If you review your life's choices, you will see where fear played a prominent role in every major decision you have ever made. For instance, if I do this, I'm rewarded. If I do that, I'm not.

"As long as the soul is submerged, the ego will play a prominent role and will direct your life through your desires and fears. The ego will literally be in control, and self-preservation and an avoidance of discomfort will be its highest objective.

"Thankfully, because of disclosure, the ego will soon play a secondary role in our lives, instead of a primary one. The heart-center will soon take over the primary role, and the head, which is essentially the ego, will get a secondary role."

John paused. "There are no words to describe the significance of this change. It changes everything. The way we perceive ourselves, the way we perceive others, the way we organize society. Our entire civilization will be adapted to this new meme.

"Once you begin to see how life is integrated, your choices will stop being about you, and more about us. Once you recognize that you are part of a whole, then you will become more concerned for the whole's welfare instead of your own. You will begin to live for that whole and not for yourself."

"I find that hard to believe," the interviewer said skeptically.

John laughed. "That's how it works. I'm not giving you my opinion. Awareness changes everything. Truth changes everyone. You can't go back."

"So, you are saying that now that the truth has been disclosed, humanity will begin to live differently? That the ego will take on a secondary role, and allow the heart to lead?"

John nodded. "Absolutely. It won't happen overnight, but over the next few generations, the ego will be steadily marginalized. Instead of a society dominated by egotists and narcissists, we will see a preponderance of humanitarians focused on selfless service."

The interviewer shifted in his seat, appearing to be uncomfortable, not just with the chair, but with the answers he was receiving. "Okay, you seem to have made the right prediction about religions failing. That is clearly occurring. Your explanation of air being conscious seems to fit with the disclosure that everything is one consciousness. So, I'll give you the benefit of the doubt about the ego, but I am skeptical that it is going to happen."

John grinned, but did not reply.

"I want to go back to something you said earlier. You said that we are not separate. However, aren't we different?" the interviewer asked.

"Sure, we have different souls, different personalities, and even different objectives. However, that does not make us separate."

"I don't understand. How can we be different and not be separate?"

"A good analogy is our fingers," John replied. "Your fingers are different, but they are not separate. They are part of the same body."

"But our fingers are not evolving," the interviewer said skeptically.

John smiled. "Good, I like it when I get probing questions and some push back. We can have a better conversation and dig deeper into the subject. Let's use another analogy then. The cells in your body are different, but they are not separate. Your cells are intelligent and are evolving. Some of them can prevent cancer on their own, and some of them need help from other cells, but they all coexist in the same body."

"Okay, I get your point. We are all part of the same body, the body of the Creator. And all consciousness is connected into one whole."

John nodded. "Very good. That recognition is what is creating unity consciousness on this planet as we speak. We are all starting to think similarly and are creating a new world. Our thoughts are being shared and felt by everyone. It's a democracy of thoughts and beliefs, and the outcome is going to be peace on earth."

"Isn't that just a utopian dream?"

"No, it is quite real," John replied. "The planet is evolving to higher levels of consciousness. The energy vibrations that we live in are rising. Only those who are compatible with this higher vibration will remain. This will leave a populace that is very similar with high ideals. I think the outcome is going to be very harmonious. In fact, I'm expecting a new civilization that is based on love.

"The whole purpose of Team Creator is to increase the energy vibration throughout the world. We are old soul lightworkers who hold high vibrational energy. We radiate this energy which is imbued into the mass consciousness that permeates all of life. We are uplifting the planetary energy by our thoughts and beliefs.

"What Team Creator is doing is also being done by millions of others by their thoughts and beliefs. This new disclosure will only expand that effort. As spiritual light expands and envelops more people, the world awakens. This has already started, and will only speed up from this disclosure."

"I want to go back to one of my first questions," the interviewer said. "What is the truth that has been hidden? You mentioned separation, but I think you have more to say on this subject."

John nodded. "Indeed. Some of the crucial truths that have been hidden are reincarnation and the meaning of life. Everyone on this planet, or nearly everyone, is here to evolve their soul. The average person has lived more than one hundred lives. Many of us have lived more than a thousand. But these reincarnated lives that we are currently living are mere blips of our soul's experience. Most of our soul's experience is done when we are discarnate light bodies. When we reincarnate, we do it for a specific reason, a specific lesson, and for a very short period of time.

"There is no reason to judge a fellow soul, when you have no idea what lesson they are learning. The final lesson, and where we are all heading, is to learn that we are the Creator. Once that lesson is learned, all we will want to do is live through acts of love. Many old souls are close to learning that lesson. Ultimately, we come to personify purity and innocence, along with unconditional love. Because that is the core of the Creator and the core of who we are. That is our true self.

"However, evolving the soul to reach that final lesson requires a very long journey. We end up playing hundreds or thousands of different roles. Some of them are positive, and some negative. We all go through this. So, pointing a finger at someone and judging them is naive. It is done from a lack of knowledge, a lack of wisdom."

John paused and waited for the next question.

"So, we need all of these positive and negative experiences to learn wisdom?"

John nodded. "Yes. As the saying goes, nothing compares to experience."

"Life is simply a series of lessons?" the interviewer asked skeptically.

"You could say that. We are all evolving by using experience. What are we evolving to? Let me answer that question. We are all Gods in the making. In fact, some would say that we are already Gods in the flesh. I'm in the former camp. I think we are all trying to become ascended masters. We're a long way from becoming a realized God."

The interview gave John a serious look. "That's a good topic. What's an ascended master?"

"Nearly everyone on this planet is not an ascended master. I would say there might be one thousand, but probably less. And they are only here because Earth is ascending and needs help at this time. Once you become an ascended master, you no longer have to incarnate. You would normally avoid a dense planet like Earth, because it's not compatible with your energy and evolvement.

You have evolved to the point where you can ascend to higher dimensions beyond the lower fifth dimension.

"The lower fifth dimension is where nearly all of us will go after we leave our bodies. Those fortunate enough to have evolved high enough can bypass this level and go higher. I personally would love to ascend in this lifetime and become an ascended master, but I don't think I'm quite ready. Perhaps a few more lives."

"Why do you want to ascend? Why is it so important?" the interviewer asked, with more interest than normal.

John smiled. "See, you don't know. The truth has been withheld. However, I will answer your question. Until a soul has evolved highly enough to become an ascended master, they need guidance. This guidance is performed by guardian angels and highly evolved souls who work on guidance councils. As a soul, you are assigned a counselor, who resides in the lower fifth dimension. In a way, we are stuck there until we evolve."

The interviewer nodded. "This sounds like getting stuck on the wheel of karma that the Indian Hindu religion speaks about."

"It's exactly that. There is your truth. We are all here trying to get off the wheel. That is why we subject ourselves to such difficult circumstances. This planet is a wonderful school for learning, but it can be quite harsh and difficult. In fact, it's considered courageous to incarnate on this planet."

"Tell me more about the ascended masters," the interviewer requested.

"They are the true Gods in training. They have the ultimate freedom. They can choose who will be their guides, what lessons they want to learn, where they will learn them, and which dimensions to visit. I call it the ultimate existence. Most people think they get to live one life and then go to heaven. However, true heaven is having the freedom to go anywhere and experience what you want. That is not something that is possible without spiritual evolvement."

"And that is why we are here?"

John nodded. "Exactly."

"Everyone is trying to get off the wheel and become an ascended master?"

John nodded. "Yes."

"So, it's like everyone here is in grade school and the ascended masters are in college?"

John laughed. "Not a bad analogy. A better one would be that everyone here is in kindergarten and the ascended masters are going for their second doctorate. You have to realize how difficult it is to become an ascended master. I've lived over a thousand lives and I'm still trying."

"How do you know that?" the interviewer asked, intrigued.

"Once you get closer to the end, you are given more information. What you need to know will be given to you. It's kind of like the saying, 'When the student is ready, the teacher appears.' Everyone can try to find out about their past lives, or how many there have been. However, unless you need to know, the information will be withheld."

"So, mediums? Is that how you got it?"

John nodded. "Yes, and my spirit guides."

"So, guardian angels, spirit guides, psychics, mediums, ghosts, that's all real?" the interviewer asked skeptically.

John nodded. "There are more discarnate light beings around us than there are humans. All of us have at least one guardian angel, and many have several. Also, light beings who are not our guides like to visit us. Many people can communicate with these light beings. That is how so much knowledge has been released about reincarnation and ascended masters."

"You're talking about channeled material?"

John nodded. "Yes. That is what it is called when a human communicates with a discarnate being. Sometimes, the discarnate being takes over a person's body and speaks through them. This is kind of spooky, but is quite common. I prefer mediums who can communicate directly with a discarnate light being."

"What kind of proof do you have that this channeling is real?"

John paused to think of the best reply. "There are so many examples. One of my favorites is a well-known true story. A lady was driving with her son in a rainstorm and drove off the road into a lake. A paramedic was following her and saw her car sink into the water. He swam down and rescued both of them.

"The mother was resuscitated fairly quickly and suffered no problems. The boy was also resuscitated, but went into a coma. The doctors said he had no brain activity and they wanted to remove him from the machines that were keeping him alive. His mother was contemplating what to do, when suddenly she started hearing a voice in her head.

"This voice came from a discarnate being, who gave her precise instructions on how to save her son. The doctors thought she was crazy. However, three days later, the boy made a full recovery. She told her story to the world and said she had never heard that voice in her head before the accident. There are hundreds of stories like this."

"Okay, that's a wrap. Thank you so much," the interviewer said.

"My pleasure," John said, removing the microphone from his collar.

Chapter Eight

Free Tours

After the television interview, Team Creator became a very busy place. People came from all over the country for either a healing or to visit. The visitors wanted to see for themselves that it was real. Many wanted to live here, but Gypsyland had filled up very quickly. A third community had formed a few miles in the distance and was growing at a rapid pace.

There were so many visitors that Team Creator decided to give free tours on Fridays and Saturdays. The tours began at noon and included a complete tour of Team Creator, followed by a video lecture. It lasted about one hour and was very popular. The video lecture was by John Randall and included a question and answer session after it finished. The questions were answered by someone from the youth movement.

They built a new building for the tours. It held one hundred people and had a large screen for the video lectures. It was also used at night to show movies to the Team Creator community. The chairs they installed were quite comfortable and were bolted to the floor. Each chair was separated by about six inches so that the visitors did not have to squeeze next to each other.

The youth movement was in charge of leading the tours. Each week, two people from the movement were scheduled to conduct the tours. Depending on how many visitors showed up, sometimes they would separate the visitors into two groups. For most tours, there were only enough people for one group.

Today was Sarah and Alice's day to do the tour. They showed up at the front building to welcome the visitors. Each visitor had a stick-on name tag that revealed that they had signed up for the tour. The name tags had large letters so that the tour leaders could read them. They tried to make it personal by calling the visitors by their first names. Sarah and Alice also wore clearly readable name tags. The tour leaders wore lightweight vests with the logo of Team Creator across the front. This was, essentially, their uniform. Their last two props were a whistle and a Team Creator flag, which they used to get the group's attention.

At noon, Sarah blew her whistle and waved her flag. There were about thirty visitors for this tour. A wave of the flag would have been sufficient to get their attention, but Sarah liked to blow her whistle once. She would not likely blow it again that day.

Alice stood by and let Sarah run the show. If it was a bigger crowd, they would have split it in half. Alice lingered near the group, away from Sarah, to see if anyone had questions. She found that often people were too shy to speak up unless you were right next to them.

"Hello, everyone. I'm Sarah, your tour leader today. Welcome to Team Creator." She pointed at Alice. "This is Alice. She will be helping me and can answer any questions that you have.

"Today, I'm going to give you a complete tour of Team Creator, and then we are going to go inside and watch a video lecture by John Randall. After the video, Alice will answer any questions that you have. You will get a very personal introduction into what Team Creator is all about. We hope that some of you will become members after the tour. That reminds me. Are any of you already members of Team Creator?"

Sarah waited for a reply.

One hand went up.

"Congratulations," Sarah exclaimed excitedly. "And thank you for helping to spread the light!"

Sarah then told the story of how the original members of Team Creator had moved here and built the original buildings. She explained how to become a member and how the community functioned. After talking for about ten minutes, she then proceeded to give them a tour of the property. At each stop, she would talk for about five minutes and give more details about the community, then she would answer questions that anyone had.

After about a half hour, they ended up at the new tour building for the video lecture. Everyone found a seat, and then the lights were dimmed for the video presentation. It lasted about fifteen minutes. The video explained how to become a member of Team Creator and went into detail about the hand prayer and living God's virtues. Toward the end of the video, John talked about the new memes, and how the world was changing into a place of love.

As soon as the lights were back on, Alice was standing in the front of the room behind a lectern to answer questions.

"I'm here to answer any questions that you may have about Team Creator, or what you saw in the video," Alice said.

Several people in the audience raised their hand.

She pointed at one of the visitors.

"How does the light spread? In the video, he talked about how you are spreading the light and that this light is expanding. How does that work?"

"Everyone has a soul which exists as an energy field," Alice began. "The energy field wraps around the body, and the body is contained within this field. In other words, our soul is not inside our body; it is wrapped around it. Our thoughts and beliefs determine the vibration and colors of this energy field. The higher the vibration, the more colorful and dynamic this aura becomes. The lower the vibration, the darker and listless it becomes.

"As more and more people embody God's virtues, the more their aura shines with dynamic colors. This has the effect of impacting the global mass consciousness. Thus, it has the effect of expanding the spiritual light on the planet. The aura of each individual is a potential colorful rainbow of energy. These rainbows are the spiritual light of the planet. Each rainbow of light can be considered a love energy field. Then, as love begins to expand, it steadily becomes the dominant energy. Make sense?"

Alice stopped, and another hand was raised. She pointed at the person.

"Can I create my own hand prayer, or do I need to follow something similar to what was presented in the video?"

"Of course, you can create your own. The hand prayer is just a tool to help you to follow God's virtues. Here at Team Creator, most of us no longer use the hand prayer. Instead, we know as soon as we wake up each morning that we are going to live that day through selfless service by doing acts of love. We know this because we have come to respect the Creator to such a degree that any other mode of living would be counterproductive.

"Once you have enough self-respect for your soul, and what it represents, the only behavior that makes sense are acts of love. That is how the soul evolves, and it is how humanity thrives. Anything else is in conflict with that outcome.

"To answer your question, you can create any hand prayer that you like and use it until it is no longer needed. Think of it as training wheels or a crutch. It is only a temporary tool that leads you to a new way of living."

Another hand was raised. She pointed at the person.

"Can you explain more about this new meme he talked about? And do you think it can end violence on the planet?"

"The new meme is basically a new paradigm, a new way of living, a new way of thinking. Until disclosure, we used to think that we were separate from each other. Now the world is coming to the understanding that we are all connected. Inevitably, this will lead to unity consciousness, where we all hold similar beliefs and values.

"Once enough people grasp that we are all connected, it will begin to change everything. The concept of right and wrong will need to be completely rethought. The concept of judgment will no longer apply. In its place will be unconditional love and a desire to help humanity. Thus, the new meme is that we are all family, and the paradigm shift is adapting to this new meme.

"As interconnectedness becomes more and more embedded into our culture, the degree of violence will slowly diminish. Violence will not go away overnight, but it will steadily become less visible. Eventually, it will become a rarity. I don't think that will be during our lifetime, but perhaps, the next generation.

"The new meme of interconnectedness and unity consciousness is not something that society was expecting. So, it is quite shocking and hard to grasp for most people. Team Creator is at the forefront because we were expecting it. What is happening today is that this civilization is awakening. The truth is being released, and it has to be assimilated. This will take some time, but all of us can help by becoming members of Team Creator. We can each spread the light."

"Is that what a lightworker does? Spread the light?" someone asked.

Alice nodded. "Yes, that is the most important job of a lightworker. Some would say it is our only job."

Another hand went up, and Alice pointed in that direction.

"Is there anything you miss by living here in a small community off the grid?"

Alice paused. "I would like to travel more. Living here makes it difficult to travel. I haven't been on an airplane in five years. Also, I miss the larger community interaction that I used to have when I was younger. We are a bit isolated here. However, I wouldn't trade it for a second. Living here at Team Creator feels a lot like utopia. We smile a lot around here, and there is a lot of joy. I wouldn't want to live anywhere else."

Alice scanned the audience. "Any more questions?"

Alice waited, and no one raised their hand. "Okay then, that's the end of the tour. Thanks for coming, and make sure to visit our website. If you have any other questions, you can email me."

These tours had the effect of spreading the new meme of oneness across the country. This meme was already spreading at a rapid pace, but Team Creator was adding to this impact.

* * * * *

A few months later, Sarah and Mike took a trip to Sedona. Sarah's mother told her that she should have a second reading to see if they were twin souls and soul mates. Her mother knew a medium in Sedona who could confirm what Harper had told them. They could have used a phone call for the reading, but Sarah and Mike liked the idea of a road trip to be by themselves.

They borrowed a car from Team Creator and left early in the morning. It was about a five-hour drive and would be a long day on the road. They didn't expect to get home until after dinner. It was springtime, and the weather was warm. It was a perfect day for a road trip.

Sarah did not have a driver's license yet, so Mike got to drive. They each brought their cell phones in case they had any problems. Sarah's mother packed them a lunch and suggested that they stop in Oak Creek Canyon to eat.

"Did you know that John Randall wrote a book that he never published?" Mike asked, after they got on the road.

Sarah was enjoying the scenery and almost didn't hear him. "No," she muttered.

"It's called *Countdown to Awareness*. He wrote it in 1998. I ran into Harper, and she suggested that I read it. There is a manuscript of it in the Team Creator library."

"Have you read it?" Sarah asked, glancing at Mike as he drove down the road.

"Yeah, it's pretty interesting."

"Well, we have time. Tell me about it?" Sarah asked, inquisitively.

"There is a section about relationships. He says they are really about belief systems. Each person brings a set of beliefs to the relationship. These beliefs create barriers or walls that limit the relationship and prevent couples from experiencing unconditional love. Beliefs create conditions and the relationship ends up being an agreement on which conditions must be met."

"Sort of like, you do this, and I'll do that, or otherwise a fight breaks out?" Sarah asked.

"Yeah, kind of like that. He says that conditions are really limitations. I brought the manuscript. It's in my pack on the back seat. Why don't you get it? I used a Post-it to mark some of the pages. Why don't you read them out loud?"

"Sure," Sarah replied. She unbuckled her seat belt and reached over the seat to open his backpack. Soon afterward, she was back in her seat, buckled up, with the book in her hands.

"This is cool," Sarah said, looking at the cover. "I want to read it after you are done."

"Read the pages with Post-its. There are only a few. Then we can talk about them."

"Okay," she replied, turning to the Post-it note.

Sarah paused and then began reading.

"Naked, under the sheets, I was in a blissful mood. 'Do you feel as wonderful as I do?' I asked.

She laughed. 'Yeah, an amazing sense of calm. I feel great, not a worry in the world.'

I laughed. 'My ideas are unconventional when it comes to relationships. I believe in unconditional love. Most people don't even know what the word means.'

'What does it mean, John?'

'It means no boundaries, no lines that can't be crossed. You live your life, and I live mine, and we share our lives. Does that make sense?'

'We have our independence?' Julie said. "We don't tell each other how to live. Is that what you mean?'

'Yeah. I don't like role-playing. That always creates conflict. If we try to define roles, we'll end up in a relationship based on conflict. Roles are too constrictive. I don't want to have to play a role for you, and I don't want you to play a role for me.'

'John, what do you mean by role-playing?'

I smiled. 'The way most relationships are based. People behave according to expectations. We agree to live within a set of boundaries. These boundaries are often unspoken, such as infidelity, but they are always limiting. Thus, we agree to limit our behavior. I don't want to limit your behavior or have mine limited. I don't want to play a role that is limiting.'

She grimaced. 'How can that be? Relationships are about trust and agreement, John. We can't have anarchy and expect the relationship to last. An unlimited relationship? That doesn't sound possible.'

'Sure it is. That's like saying relationships can't have freedom. Of course, it's possible. It's the ultimate relationship. It's unconditional love. It's how two people share their lives. Today, most people don't share their lives. Instead, they agree to restrict their lives together. Conditional love is based on restrictions and boundaries that create role-playing. It's a setup for conflict.'

'Interesting. Tell me more,' she said.

'I want you to perceive me as free to live my life as I desire, with you as a part of it. I want us to share our lives. I don't want you to have to conform to a role I determine in my head. I don't want to restrict you. Let me give you an example. Say this talk never occurred. Instead, we talked about your life and my life and how we currently live. From this talk, we would form images of how we currently live. Then we would date and reinforce these images. I would accept you for your current way of living, and you would accept me for mine. Based on these images, we would define roles we thought were acceptable. We would draw boundaries based on these images, and an inherent conflict would form.'

'What kind of conflict?' she asked.

'Say I leave town with a friend without telling you. In your mind, this is a boundary not to be crossed. When I return, you are furious because I crossed an imagined boundary. I didn't get permission, which you assume is a requirement for our relationship.'

'That's common courtesy,' she said confidently.

'No, that's control. People in relationships are constantly controlling each other. Without freedom in a relationship, we can't have unconditional love.'

Julie pondered. 'Hmm, that's interesting. We allow each other the freedom to do what we want? Tell me more.'

'Boundaries are limiting and restrict our freedom. They are created for one purpose: to control each other. Most boundaries are very subtle and rarely discussed until they are crossed. For instance, I recently read in the newspaper that a marriage dissolved because of a pizza order. The husband ordered a pizza the wife didn't like, and she divorced him.'

'She was just looking for an excuse,' Julie said.

'Maybe, but she found a boundary to use as an excuse. She created the boundary, and he had no idea the boundary would determine his marriage. See how it works? When we each define roles and boundaries, conflict is built-in to the relationship. Conflicts are traps ready to spring. We set them for each other.'

'John, conflict is pretty hard to avoid.'

'I agree. But it's the boundaries that make conflict inevitable. If we can limit or eliminate the boundaries, we can avoid conflict.'

'I don't know if that's possible,' Julie said.

'You think we have to control each other?'

She laughed. 'That's the way it is. That's human nature.'

'I disagree. I think it's a conditioned behavior taught to us. We don't have to control each other. I don't plan on controlling you.'

She hesitated. 'Part of me wants to listen to your crazy philosophy, and another part of me wants to ignore you. Your ideas are either inspiring or insanity. I haven't made up my mind which way I feel.'

'Sometimes I feel like I'm wasting my time, Julie. If it wasn't for the fact that civilization is nearing a transition, I would be very frustrated. My crazy philosophy *is* the future. Today, conflict dominates society. That has to change. Ninety-five percent of relationships are based on role-playing and boundaries. Once we draw a boundary in our mind, the relationship is based on conditional love, on *conditions*, and the boundaries are the conditions. We're going to need freedom in our relationships if we're going to have freedom in society.'

Julie laughed. 'You're deep, John. I understand what you're saying, but it's so extreme! If I give you your freedom, it means you can also do whatever you want.'

'Yeah, but it also means I'll allow you to do whatever you want. If you love someone, set them free...' I waited for her response.

'I need at least one boundary.'

'Sure, what is it?' John asked.

'I don't want you to have sex with other women.'

'Okay, let's put up that boundary. I can't see myself having sex with other women anyway.'

Julie looked at me skeptically. 'It seems risky not having boundaries. I've always controlled the men in my life to a certain extent. I've never given a man a free pass to do whatever he wants. But maybe you're right. Maybe that's why it never worked and why I never had a satisfying relationship. When I look at my friends' marriages, they're mostly frustrated. I see them giving more than they get back. Maybe your idea is worth a try.'

'One thing, Julie, I don't think I'm going to have sex with other women. But that isn't a stipulation I'll put on you, though. You're free to do as you please.'

'Where did you get these ideas?' she asked incredulously.

I laughed. 'Too much reading, I guess. Seriously, once we become aware that we are eternal, constrictions on human relationships become limiting. So, I thought, why live in conflict? Why not live in freedom? Why not choose unconditional love? You're free, Julie, and I won't take that from you. Be who you want to be and let me hang around and enjoy your presence. If you tire of me, I'll leave. Just point to the door and tell me to get out. Until then, I'll savor our relationship. I'll feel blessed that I'm in your life.' I smiled.

Julie laughed, then kissed and held me. 'You are too much.' She looked at me. 'I mean that in a good way. I feel exhilarated. You're what I've been looking for, John, but never expected.'

'I'm glad you found me.' I kissed her back."

Sarah stopped reading and glanced at Mike. "That's interesting stuff. So, what he is implying is that we have to be careful on which conditions we place on each other."

Mike nodded. "Also, we have to be careful not to keep these conditions secret from each other."

Sarah smiled. "True. I didn't think of that. I might secretly dislike some of your behaviors and never tell you. This can steadily build up until it becomes a condition determining if I like you or not anymore."

Mike laughed. "That better not happen."

"I'll make sure to tell you what I don't like."

"Or, better yet, you can just like everything that I do."

Sarah laughed. "Fat chance, buddy."

"Oh, no. Here come the conditions and we're not even married yet."

Sarah laughed again. "We can try to reduce the conditions as much as possible, but I agree with Julie. It's not very practical."

"So, you're saying that unconditional love isn't for us?"

Sarah paused. "Hmm. We'll work on it."

"By the way, when do you want to get married," Mike asked pragmatically.

"Have you thought about it?" Sarah replied.

"Sure. Haven't you?"

Sarah nodded. "I was thinking my eighteenth birthday. Is that too soon?"

"No, that sounds perfect," Mike replied pragmatically.

Sarah started laughing. "This is crazy. We just decided to get married and you haven't even asked me yet."

Mike laughed. "Well, it's destiny. We both want it. Why do I need to get on one knee?"

"Yeah, you're right. We already practically told our parents we are getting married."

Mike glanced at Sarah. "I need to get you a ring."

"Do you have your dad's credit card?" Sarah asked.

Mike nodded.

"Let's go shopping for a ring in Sedona," Sarah said.

"My parents will kill me," Mike said.

"No, worst case, we take it back. What do you think those odds are?"

Mike laughed. "Pretty low."

"We won't spend a lot. I don't need a big diamond ring," Sarah said.

"Okay, we'll do it."

Free Tours - Chapter Eight

* * * * *

They drove down Oak Creek Canyon and stopped in an area with a good view of the creek. The red rocks and oak trees in the canyon were stunningly beautiful. They were only about thirty minutes from Sedona. Inside the packed lunch was a blanket, which they spread out on the green grass. They smiled at each other as they ate their lunch, without a care in the world.

"This is the most beautiful place I think I have ever been to before," Sarah said.

"You haven't seen Sedona yet," Mike said.

"Today is the best day of my life so far," Sarah said.

"Yeah, it's high on my list too."

"I can't keep from thinking about what John said about relationships and unconditional love. I'm glad we are getting married young so that we won't have much baggage. Most millennials get married late and must have a lot of baggage."

"Yeah, from what I've read, the divorce rate is about fifty percent," Mike said.

"I wonder if it is related to the boundaries that people put up and the conditions they force each other to live by."

"Probably," Mike said. "I think John makes a good case that conditional love is very difficult to maintain. There's always a conflict ready to break out if a condition is crossed. People are literally forcing each other to behave. The little freedom that exists is probably only obtained infrequently."

"That sounds so dreadful," Sarah said unhappily.

"Well, if we allow each other freedom and a lack of conditions, then we can be happy together."

Sarah smiled. "Agreed."

They were both quiet.

"I'm going to have to read that book carefully," Sarah said.

Mike smiled. "We'll figure it out."

Sarah smiled. "Yeah, I think we will."

Mike looked up at the red canyon walls. "This seems like the perfect place to meditate."

"Do you meditate?" Sarah asked.

"I used to when I was fourteen, but John taught us how to merge with our soul. Once you get close enough to your soul, it becomes part of your life."

"What do you mean?" Sarah asked, intrigued.

"It's a melding. You open up your soul channel and keep it open. You integrate it into your life. Once you merge with your soul, there is no reason to meditate anymore."

Sarah stared at Mike. "I want to learn how."

Mike smiled. "Sure, I'll teach you. After you do the hand prayer in the morning, open up your soul channel and keep it open."

"You mean keep your mind as quiet as you can?" Sarah said with uncertainty.

"Sort of. What you want to do is keep the channel open. In other words, even now as we are speaking, I have another layer of consciousness that is listening to my soul. All I have to do is pay attention to it. I can listen and speak at the same time. Does that make sense?"

Sarah hesitated. "Oh! I see what you mean by keeping the channel open. Even if we speak, we can still listen to the soul. Even if we think, we can still listen. We just have to always be aware of its existence. If we pay attention to the channel, it never closes."

Mike smiled. "You're a fast learner."

Sarah laughed. "Girls are smarter than boys."

Free Tours - Chapter Eight

* * * * *

The rest of the day continued to be magical. The reading was a success, with everything that Harper had told them confirmed. They walked around Sedona shopping for an engagement ring. Sedona was built in what could be considered a national park. The surrounding magnificent red rocks created a beautiful backdrop to the small town. It was a tourist center, with hundreds of shops. It didn't take long for Sarah to find something beautiful that she liked. Then, once her ring finger had an engagement ring firmly ensconced, they walked around town enjoying the rest of the day.

After a couple of hours, they got back on the road for the five-hour return trip. Normally, this would have been a bit monotonous, but they were so happy that it was nothing else but sheer joy.

Chapter Nine

TED TALK

The next week, John was invited to give a Ted Talk. These were provided to the public on the website www.ted.com. Their slogan was, "Ideas worth sharing." He wanted to turn it down because the Ted Talks were part of the societal culture he was trying to break down and replace. However, he gave in because of the vast audience it would receive and the opportunity to spread the word of Team Creator. His topic was the new memes.

John stepped onto the stage. He had a wireless microphone that was wrapped around the back of his head and held on using his ears. The stage was well-lit, along with the audience. As he scanned the full house, he was met with a polite ovation, which he waited to subside.

"Hi, I'm John Randall, one of the founders of Team Creator. Tonight, I'm going to talk about the new memes that are spreading across the world, and how these memes are going to solve all of our problems."

John paused to see how the audience reacted to his implausible statement.

"First of all, what is the most significant new meme? I would submit that it is the idea that we are all consciously connected. That there is no separation between us. This meme leads to other memes that are proliferating. Such as, if there is only one consciousness that we share, wouldn't that consciousness be God, the Creator?"

John paused again and scanned the crowd to emphasize his point.

"This leads to the next meme, which is that we are one with God, and thus eternal. Oh boy, doesn't this open up all kinds of new memes into society? Such as reincarnation, other planes of existence, and our relationship to the Creator. And what about right and wrong? If God is perfect, and we are one with God, aren't we also perfect?"

John paused. "Okay, that's all of the questions I am going to ask you tonight. Now I'm going to talk about how these new memes are going to solve our problems. First of all, words, ideas, and analysis can never solve problems. I learned that from Krishnamurti. He said that thought can never solve a problem, and he was right. I'm not talking about problems that have defined solutions, such as a plumbing problem or a power outage. I'm talking about problems that humanity has been trying to solve for millennia, such as how do we cure poverty, or how do we prevent violence and wars.

"This is why we cannot legislate solutions or use words in constitutional documents to solve big problems. We've tried that and all it seems to do is lead to the degradation of society. It doesn't work. Thoughts, words, ideas, concepts, analysis, these will never create solutions.

"In fact, ideas and ideologies only create conflict. Instead of creating solutions, they create more problems. There is another way to provide solutions, but this requires another way of looking at life, another way of living.

"The solution only occurs by removing the problem from your mind. It has to no longer exist as part of your mindset. This is similar to the concept of out of sight, out of mind. However, removing problems from your mind is not easy to do, because you have to free your mind from all of the ideas and social conditioning that have created the problem. The thing we have to acknowledge is that the reason problems exist is because we have created them. We have allowed them to exist.

"The starting place for solving a problem is deciding which thoughts get to stay. This is a process of surrendering. You are surrendering your ego identity to something more, which is a connection to the Creator. You do this by living God's virtues, and these get to stay in your mind. Once only virtues are left, your problems are resolved.

"We all know God's virtues: kindness, caring, being considerate, compassionate, humble, grateful, trusting, faithful, selfless, innocence, unconditional love, and acts of love. When you live these in the present moment, then all problems are resolved.

"These are objective truths. Another objective truth is that truth is always true. All virtues are objective truth. They are always true. The Creator is real. Another objective truth. Our soul is real. Another objective truth. There is only one consciousness. Again, another objective truth. We are the generation that gets to create a new paradigm, a new era, a new wave, whatever you want to call it, that is based on objective truth."

John passed for effect.

"These are ideas that we will hold, and everything else will be forgotten."

John paused and scanned the room to emphasize his point.

"By freeing your mind of ideologies and cultural conditioning that are based on falsehoods, you have the freedom to start over. This is incredibly releasing. People have no idea how trapped they have been by their false beliefs and false thoughts. They have literally imprisoned in their minds. I am here to free you.

"God's virtues are not concepts. Love, virtue, innocence. These are not constructs that we have created. They are who we are. They are either true or false. The mind does not get trapped by virtues.

"This is where the solutions appear. When you focus on living these virtues, you have time to clear your mind and become observant. Anything that pops into your head that is not in alignment with these virtues is discarded.

"At first this is difficult, as the ego fights for its identity. The ego will try to push your buttons and get you to focus on either the past or the future. The ego's favorite button is fear, but it can also use pleasure quite effectively. Your job is to marginalize the ego and keep your mind quiet.

"It may appear to be ludicrous, or even unnatural, to attempt to marginalize the ego. However, freedom only exists without the prison of your thoughts, which can be any form of ego self-preservation. True freedom is to live in the present moment without any fixation on thoughts that are based on some type of past or future event."

John took a few steps to the left and talked to that side of the room.

"Religions, ideologies, and cultural norms are quite mischievous. They are mental traps that take away both the freedom of thought and our true connection to God, the Creator. If we don't have the same religion, ideologies, or beliefs, then a division arises between us. A potential conflict arises. A false conflict, an illusion.

"Krishnamurti called this 'freedom from the known.' The known are the concepts that we tend to rely on to make our decisions. These concepts also tend to invade our thoughts and take over our minds. We have to neuter these concepts and embrace the freedom that exists apart from concepts and ideologies and rely only on objective truth.

"The only concepts to embrace are acts of love and the virtues of God. All other concepts, we need to keep on a tight leash and keep them out of our thoughts. In fact, try to keep your mind as quiet and silent as possible. This is where freedom and harmony flourish.

"Another new meme is that political ideologies no longer matter. In fact, we no longer want to embrace societal norms, concepts of right and wrong, or even judgments of people. Instead, we want to embrace compassion and humanity. These are God's virtues, and they take us away from current social norms.

"We have tried to codify freedom through our constitutional documents of words, but clearly, it has failed. Instead, we have witnessed society degrade over the last generation to where freedom has lost its meaning. Now, this degradation is reversing because of disclosure, and the fact that the Constitution, religions, and social concepts are losing their potency. In their place, is a new meme of interconnectedness and love.

"No moral standard, no government document, can bring us together in peace. No central authority can legislate peace and freedom. This is obvious if you look closely at history. The only solution is that each individual must become his or her own moral authority, with a foundation of objective truth. From this knowledge, one can live God's virtues and not judge others by societal norms that dictate moral standards."

John paused to emphasize his point.

"There are several things that change people's behavior and bring about solutions to our problems. Sometimes, it is knowledge, such as knowing that something is dangerous. Sometimes, it is experience, such as a bad experience, that you do not want to repeat. However, for most people, change is difficult. That is the purpose of the hand prayer. It is a tool that helps people to marginalize their ego until they understand that love is not found in the ego.

"For some people, surrendering their ego identity and embracing their heart is too difficult. They are not ready yet. However, with disclosure, vast numbers of people are ready to identify with their soul and embrace a new way of living. This is what will lead to solutions. They will purge their minds of old problems, which will fall away like they never existed.

"If you are going to find peace in your heart, that can only happen if you get close to your soul. This can only be done with a quiet mind and an alignment with what the soul embodies, which are God's virtues. This alignment can also be obtained from acts of love and other virtues of God.

"One of the most important things to understand is that everyone's truth is different. This is what creates compassion and leads to selfless service. Ultimately, selfless service is what we will all want to do, but this is not achieved overnight. It can take many lifetimes to come to this conclusion."

John paused and moved back to the center to the stage.

"The new memes are going to change how we look at each other and how we perceive one another. Instead of judging one another through either past experiences or cultural assumptions, we will begin to see each individual as a larger soul that we can't completely recognize. We will begin to recognize that there is more to an individual than meets the eye.

"The soul is going to come alive through perception. This is perhaps the biggest meme that is now passing through humanity. People are beginning to recognize the impact the soul has on their lives, and how it can be accessed through a quiet mind.

"Another important thing to know is that truth cannot be shared because words do not encompass truth. Truth is only found within, and truth is more than words. In fact, the truth is a combination of many memes, with each meme meaning something different to each person. For this reason, truth is very difficult to share.

"Truth is a big word and encompasses how we each define the Creator. No two people can define the Creator the same way. This is why truth cannot be explained with words. However, this does not mean that objective truth does not exist.

"What is occurring on the planet at this time are the initial urges toward selfless service for all of humanity to exemplify. This is one of the new memes, although it is only being felt on a small scale at this time. Steadily, people will get out of their egos, out of their ideologies, out of their religions, and feel from their hearts. Love and compassion will begin to manifest.

"The civilization that we are creating is not about individualism. No, that is the past. The future is about humanity and freedom. It won't be much longer before we get rid of money, and everyone will have what they need. Food and shelter will not be a problem for anyone on this planet for much longer.

"A move away from ego to the heart will solve all of our problems. You may doubt that it is possible for people to surrender their ego to their heart. However, that is what the new memes will achieve. Now that people are aware that not only is the soul real, but that it is connected to all of life, it will change people.

"There will be a recognition of how to tap into the soul, and that it can only be done by marginalizing the ego. The mind will be purified and cleansed, as ideologies are removed and no longer have any power over people. It will be similar to when you find a poisonous spider in your house. You remove it. Or, if you hear a rattlesnake near you, then you step away. These are two examples of the mind reacting to what it knows to be the right thing to do. There is no gray area. You know immediately the right outcome.

"This is how you will marginalize the ego. If your mind is trapped in cultural norms of the past, they will be purged. There will be no gray area when it comes to respecting the Creator. Who comes first, the ego or the Creator? Who comes first, the personality identity or the soul identity?"

John paused, scanning the audience to see if anyone was grasping his message. He could not tell, so he continued.

"Frustration, fear, anxiety all originate in the ego. It is the ego's desire to control its environment and its destiny. The ego always wants to control what is going to happen next. When you flip that dynamic and let the Creator and the soul come first, the only thing that matters is the present moment, because that is where the soul is accessible. Thought has to subside for the soul to come through. The minute you connect with your soul, at that time, frustration, fear, and anxiety dissipate. The mere recognition that the soul exists is an act of rebellion toward the ego.

"Solutions to our problems will happen automatically as people become more connected to their soul. This will happen by the awareness of the soul. The only way to be aware is to have a quiet, silent mind, which allows you to connect with your soul. Once connected, the soul becomes your eyes and ears. This connection allows you to become observant of your mind, and highly alert. In this state of mind, the ego is held at bay. Unvirtuous thoughts are quickly discarded. At Team Creator, we call this staying heart-centered.

"You have to be highly alert to do this, but it is possible. It works like this. You do the hand prayer to align yourself with God's virtues. Once you are aligned, your mind becomes heart-centered. You are good to go. As the day progresses, your ego will try to get your attention and pull you into thinking unvirtuous thoughts. Once these arise, you quickly get out of your head and into your heart and allow these thoughts to dissipate. The more observant and alert you are of your thoughts, the more you will be able to stay heart-centered.

"When you are observing yourself carefully, you can monitor any deviation from virtue. Steadily, you will learn how to keep unvirtuous thoughts out of your life. Then you will be living God's virtues at all times and living through acts of love. It will begin to become the norm. Deviation then becomes rare, if it happens at all.

"As you can imagine, living a virtuous life can initially be demanding. A commitment must be made. An allegiance to the Creator must be taken. A decision to subvert the ego's will for the Creator's will must be followed. This is a surrendering process.

"After this decision is made, then you have to marginalize the ego through observing the self. This requires being attentive, which is very difficult to do. It is hard to be alert and aware of your thoughts and actions at all times, because the mind wants to be busy. This is called self-observation, and it only works when the mind is quiet, and the heart is alert. When you consciously become attentive, observant of yourself through the heart, at that moment, your thoughts stop. Once your thoughts stop, you can be attentive to any thoughts that arise, and those thoughts can be observed. If they are virtuous, then you act. If they are unvirtuous, then you should pay them no mind."

John paused and walked to the right side of the stage.

"In the London subways, they have signs that say, 'Mind the gap.' This basically means to pay attention to the gap in the floor between the platform and the train. They don't want anyone to trip. When you are observing yourself, you need to mind the unvirtuousness. You don't want to trip. That is the key to keeping in alignment with the soul. It keeps the connection open.

"Being observant of the mind is not normally how people live. People are used to living on autopilot, letting their ego tell them what to do. However, that is changing because mindfulness is now required to connect to the soul. The soul requires a quiet mind to be heard. The more observant we become, the closer to the soul we become.

"This true, hard fact is what will change humanity. Why? Because unless you know your soul, you will no longer be allowed to live on this planet. I do not know the timeframe for when this rule will take effect, but the day is quickly approaching. For this reason, I suggest that you pay attention to the last few minutes of this lecture."

John paused to see if anyone was snickering.

"When one is working, they must pay attention to the task at hand. This generally requires a preoccupation with the task. There is nothing wrong with this. As you do your task, the soul will simply leave you alone, or perhaps give you a few subtle hints if you need help. However, where people go astray, is that when they are performing a task, they allow the mind to wander. This is where the ego leads you astray. So, focus on the task at hand, or keep the mind quiet in an alert state.

"Working is a form of constant meditation. If you can focus on a task, then you do not allow the ego-mind to wander. The ego's playground is wandering into the past or the future. Don't go there unless you need to. Living in the past or the future is oxygen to the ego, and it wants to breathe. Your job is to make it pass out from a lack of oxygen. This will mean that the soul is in charge.

"If you have a difficult time keeping your mind from wandering, then do either of two things. First, try to keep your mind busy doing specific tasks. That can be working, reading, playing games, watching videos, exercising, or walking in nature. These are escapes for keeping the mind occupied, but they are not the ideal method. Ideally, you want to remain alert with a quiet mind, observing yourself. This is why there is a second method.

"The second method is to meditate at least once a day for at least ten minutes. This method teaches you how to stay alert, observing yourself and your thoughts. In the East, they meditate more than we do, especially in India, where spirituality is more prevalent. In the West, we tend to ignore meditation, but this will start to change.

"For the mind to be capable of connecting to the soul, it has to be free of obstacles. The first obstacle is a busy mind. If you are worrying about the past or the future, then the soul is blocked. If you are caught up in ideology, religious dogma, or other forms of social conditioning, then the mind is always busy. In these situations, the soul is hindered and stymied.

"To solve our problems, we all need to live virtuous lives. This requires that the mind becomes free of obstacles. This is what the new memes are all about. They are helping us to clear the obstacles. We are all getting into contact with our true selves, which is within. We are learning how to shut off the ego and quiet the mind, and perhaps most importantly, we are learning how to listen to each other. Right now, as I give this lecture, many of you are getting blocked by your built-in obstacles. However, others in this room are hearing what I am saying, and it is resonating. They are removing their obstacles, such as the cultural norms they have lived by for many years. They are recognizing that these norms are no longer valid.

"Love, virtue, innocence. These are concepts that cannot be denied. They are real. They are not human constructs or ideologies. These are the basis of our new emerging civilization. God's virtues are real. They are not beliefs or ideologies. You either live by them, or you don't. It's a true or false question, and one that you will take with you after this life is completed. These truths are what is going to transform humanity, and like I have said repeatedly, our problems will solve themselves. Once we change, the problems will no longer exist.

"Let me give you some examples of how people will change. Soon, more people will exhibit a frequency of love. This manifests when you accept everything that happens in your life as a blessing, or an opportunity. Why would you do this? Because you will begin to recognize that everything is perfection, because the Creator only knows perfection. Thus, you live with constant gratitude, and nothing can shake you from this mindset. You will live with a sense of neutrality and unconditional love at all times.

"People will begin to recognize that the more you love yourself, the more it is reflected back to you. Moreover, the higher you align to this idea, the more your aura shines light. We call this spreading the light at Team Creator.

"People will begin to recognize that our beliefs create our reality. Our beliefs create our tone, our frequency. Each individual is responsible for their tone, and thus are responsible for their individual lives. For instance, you can have the belief of either, what if something bad happens, or what if something good happens? Both are beliefs, but only one is aligned with truth. Why is that? Because the Creator, the Divine, only knows perfection, unlimitedness, success, joy, wellness, eternalness. The Creator and fear cannot coexist. So, when we think that something bad can happen, we are simply creating an idea that is false, and it can only lead us to lessons that will eventually lead us to the truth. In other words, false beliefs just take us around in circles.

"So, thoughts, actions that are false only pull us down. And we do this to ourselves by ignoring God's virtues. We literally create these outcomes via our beliefs. Change your beliefs, change the outcome.

"All problems manifest from the denial of the divine. That's quite a statement, and it's true. It's not my opinion. It's an objective truth. People think they are separate from Source, but they are not. We are all connected to Source. We are all connected to each other. This is why to judge another, to damn another, is to damn yourself. Why? Isn't the answer obvious? Yes, it is obvious, and this is why everything I have said tonight makes sense, and why humanity is about to undergo a transformation of epic proportions. The truth has been released."

John paused and bowed. "Thank you."

The crowd politely applauded.

The Hand Prayer

(Long version)

Thumb. Who do you serve? Where is your allegiance? The ego or the soul? Serve the Creator. Serve the soul. Serve humanity.

Index finger. Be an example. Remove the darkness from the world by spreading light and love. Remove the injustice and unfairness. Remove the pain and suffering. Do this by spreading light.

Middle finger. Live a life of integrity, purity, and innocence. List any habits or behaviors that you want to refrain from experiencing. Live with gratitude. Show this by being the best version of yourself.

Ring finger. Treat others with unconditional love. Be kind, caring, considerate, and compassionate.

Pinky. Be committed to spreading the light. Do this by living God's virtues of being humble, grateful, trusting, faithful, and selfless. Live with integrity.

www.ingramcontent.com/pod-product-compliance
Lightning Source LLC
Chambersburg PA
CBHW070620300426
44113CB00010B/1599